MW00480342

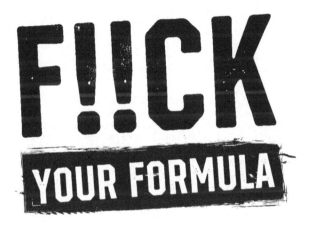

F!!CK YOUR FORMULA

Why Following Rules Is the Worst Marketing Decision You'll Ever Make

Aaron Perlut and Brian Cross
with Dominic Vaiana

F!!K Your Formula

Why Following Rules Is the Worst Marketing Decision You'll Ever Make
Aaron Perlut and Brian Cross with Dominic Vaiana
Elastic Media

Published by Elastic Media, St. Louis, MO
Copyright ©2020 Aaron Perlut & Brian Cross
All rights reserved.

No part of this publication may be reproduced, stored in a retrieval system, or transmitted in any form or by any means, electronic, mechanical, photocopying, recording, scanning, or otherwise, except as permitted under Section 107 or 108 of the 1976 United States Copyright Act, without the prior written permission of the Publisher. Requests to the Publisher for permission should be addressed to Permissions Department, Elastic Media, info@elasticmedia.com.

Limit of Liability/Disclaimer of Warranty: While the publisher and author have used their best efforts in preparing this book, they make no representations or warranties with respect to the accuracy or completeness of the contents of this book and specifically disclaim any implied warranties of merchantability or fitness for a particular purpose. No warranty may be created or extended by sales representatives or written sales materials. The advice and strategies contained herein may not be suitable for your situation. You should consult with a professional where appropriate. Neither the publisher nor author shall be liable for any loss of profit or any other commercial damages, including but not limited to special, incidental, consequential, or other damages.

Editor: Bill Motchan

Cover Design: Elasticity

Illustrations: Elasticity

Interior Design: Davis Creative Publishing Partners, DavisCreative.com

Library of Congress Cataloging-in-Publication Data

Library of Congress Control Number: 2019916526

Aaron Perlut and Brian Cross with Dominic Vaiana
F!!K Your Formula: Why Following Rules Is the
    Worst Marketing Decision You'll Ever Make
ISBN: 978-1-7334926-0-7 (Hardback)
        978-1-7334926-1-4 (Paperback)
        978-1-7334926-2-1 (eBook)

Library of Congress subject headings:

1. Business / Marketing / General-BUS043000   2. Business / Public
    Relations-BUS052000   3. Business / Advertising & Promotion-
    BUS002000

2020

Random quote inserted to appear thoughtful or as to having great depth of personality.

Contents

Introduction(s)

Given the title of this book, we owe you a good answer to the looming, ironic question bubbling up in your head: Why would two founders of a marketing agency write a book telling you to avoid marketing formulas like the plague (and call bullshit on people who peddle them)?

To answer that question, let's pay a visit to the business aisle of your local bookstore or Amazon's vast library of business books. Look closely at the marketing best-sellers and you'll notice a pattern. Many of them are written in a "how-to" format: step-by-step guides, processes, and blueprints. The authors trumpet their accomplishments and exclusive insights in a few hundred pages that are front-loaded with a few cool stories and padded with useless fluff. We even know an author (he shall remain nameless) who admitted his ideas could be condensed into a single page.

But the formulas don't end with books. Google will give you more than a quarter billion (with a "b") results when you type "marketing formula" into your search bar. Facebook, Twitter, Instagram, and LinkedIn are all littered with step-by-step marketing guides and "quick tips" that are almost always taken out of context. The podcast industry is laden with marketing fortune-tellers, prophets, soothsayers, and hucksters who are desperate to bestow their brilliant marketing strategies to audiences of eager listeners.

The formulaic cycle typically goes something like this:

1. Propagate a concept through a series of blogs and social media posts

2. Aggregate said content into a book with boring cover

3. Leverage said book into speaking engagements

4. Materialize $100 bills used for high quality plastic surgery and a 2,500-square-foot addition on second home on the Maryland Eastern Shore

Excuse us while we engage in synchronized vomiting.

By fall of 2019, we'd lost our collective shit and had enough of the empty promises and salespeople masquerading as marketing experts, which have unleashed a slew of disastrous consequences (not to mention costing gullible senior managers money, time and quite possibly their jobs). Eager entrepreneurs are being taken advantage of by slick marketing consultants. Universities are breeding herds of automatons who shy away from challenging their textbooks. Even C-suites are being seduced by the finely-crafted bullshit that's pumped out on a daily basis.

We felt obliged to put our feet down, draw a line in the sand, and a variety of other euphemisms suggesting that we wanted to end the madness once and for all, even at the risk of delegitimizing the marketing industry that's worth upwards of a trillion dollars. If there's one thing we've learned after half a century of combined experience, it's that there is no one-size-fits-all approach to marketing. There can't be. If marketing, by its very nature, is about differentiation, how can anybody expect to stand out by sharing the same cookie cutters with everyone else?

It's never been easier to be average. If you can't muster up the patience, energy, or desire to come up with customized solutions, you can simply copy and paste from your favorite book, blog, Ted Talk, or podcast. And so can everyone else—like a standup comic who rips off other routines and pimps them as their own. Few marketers acknowledge this, and fewer (perhaps none) have written a book about it—until now.

Is it a contradiction to write a marketing book explaining why many marketers are full of shit? That will be up to you to decide. But before we dive in, we need to introduce ourselves so you know who the hell is saying what as we move forward.

Greetings, upright mammals. I'm Aaron Perlut: baconist, fist-bump inventor, and indeed, my hair and beard are *that* luscious in real life. For some 25 years (damn I'm old) I've cobbled together a range of experiences in journalism, public relations and digital marketing. My career started in television but that really, really sucked. Hence, I fell into brand reputation, working for agencies and large corporations. All the while I've maintained a foothold in journalism with digital footprints at HuffingtonPost (under my maiden name), Forbes, ESPN, TechCrunch, AdWeek, BroBible, the American Mustache Institute (uh, yep) and now, this thing you're holding in your hands (considering throwing out) or viewing on a tablet. There are obviously a lot more lucrative and easier things I could've done besides tackling this book project. But alas, here we are, so let me give you the gist of *F*** Your Formula*.

Throughout the annals of history, fear has driven more destructive behavior than historians can keep up with. Racism stems from fear. Intolerance stems from fear. Unwillingness to pick up a guitar despite loving it until age 47—yes, fear. And of course, stagnation is more often than not driven by the fear of change—just ask Kodak!

Humans are also, oftentimes, lazy. Many of us are wired to find any shortcut, pattern or formula that can minimize the amount of effort required to accomplish an objective. This mindset is great for grocery shopping and unclogging toilets, but when it bleeds into creative endeavors like building a brand, the results are overwhelmingly underwhelming at best.

You've seen the headlines before:

10 tips guaranteed to boost your conversion rate by 10 percent!

5 steps to a content marketing plan that works wonders!

We found the formula to go viral on YouTube!

Sweet merciful *Chuck Norris' Armpit Muscles* people! These promises are as seductive as Trey Songz, but much like his music career, they aren't sustainable. Think about it: The sheer volume of how-to marketing advice is proof in itself that they don't work. If they did, we'd all use them and move on with the rest of our days. Truthfully, these formulas are excuses for not doing the hard work of paving your own path.

And yet, nearly all marketing "experts," "influencers" or "gurus" have one thing in common: They peddle formulas. These might work wonders for them or a small subset of people—but they're not universally applicable by a long shot. After more than two decades of navigating the marketing biz, I've discovered a nice, juicy factoid: *Formulas don't work*. They suck. In fact, brands often thrive the most when they work up the courage to throw out their old rule books.

There are two kinds of people in this world—those who adapt and those who fail. As technology continues to disrupt what we once thought to be the status quo, the future of marketing will belong to those who have the courage to take off their blinders, unplug their ears, and admit that their patterns of thinking are flawed.

We could beat on our rippling pectorals or talk until we're blue in the face about the work our agency has done for clients, but we didn't write this book to pimp our agency (partial fib number one). We wrote this book to call bullshit on everyone from new-age social media gurus to starch-shirted conformists who claim they know what's best for everyone else. We wrote this book to let brands, agencies, students and everyone else in on a big marketing secret: *There is no big secret*. And most importantly, we wrote this book to let you, the reader, know that there's always a better way.

Look, I get it: Formulas are hard to challenge. Just think of EBITA, Six Sigma or 10x Marketing. They are cooked up by armies of experts and reinforced by their millions of followers. Who are you to challenge the "best practices?" While rocking the boat might make you seasick at first, we'll explain how untangling the wires in your brain and challenging those sacred assumptions are the most crucial skills a marketer can develop.

So, next time you're sitting around your office dreaming about yoga or yogurt or Yoda or whatever, ask yourself if you should unlearn all those marketing formulas before you waste your time and money.

That little icon is me, Brian Cross. Yeah, the bald guy. Prior to co-founding Elasticity, I cut my teeth at FleishmanHillard where I was at the helm of its digital practice. "Global Practice Group Lead, Digital," I think the actual title was. It was me and a guy from London running 36 offices in eight countries trying desperately to get the Titanic to understand digital communications. Fun times. Fast forward a couple of decades, and I've had the privilege to work with brands such as AT&T, Yahoo!, Papa John's, Visa, Bud Light, Fireball, the US Treasury, nonprofits and startups alike. I've built a Swiss army knife of specialties during that time, from creative and digital strategy, to agency operations, *Top Gun* quotes, and making a mean slab of dry-rubbed ribs. I've also been an active mentor and investor in early stage technology companies and serve as their fractional CEO and marketing advisor.

I've had friends, colleagues and coworkers prodding me for years to write a book. I'm usually "the talker" in social settings and I have more ideas than I know what to do with, so naturally I was up for the challenge of translating my thoughts into a book. But what book?

As you read in the introduction to our introductions, I was sick and tired of the trite marketing strategies (if you can call a list of tactics an actual strategy) which inevitably cause audiences to become saturated with mundane, thoughtless work on behalf of brands and agencies who don't give a damn about challenging themselves. Couple that with the fact that I left "the big agency with real clients" to help build an agency predicated on stretching boundaries, and out pops the idea for *F*** Your Formula.*

I can understand the flood of formulas from a pure psychological perspective. Human beings are wired to think in a linear fashion and follow the path of least resistance, which is exactly what these books promise. Executives who come from an operations background are often convinced every process can be improved and enhanced, whether it be a call center, warehouse or R&D function. But you and I both know that history, marketing or otherwise, is defined by people who wrote their own rulebook instead of obeying the one prescribed to them. With that in mind, why would anyone ever settle for lame excuses such as, "We've always done it that way," or "That's just how we do things around here?"

Finding a better way is our call. It was when we founded Elasticity in 2009, and it always will be. I'm obsessed with solving problems, regardless of the means necessary to do so, and I don't believe in templated solutions. It takes a special person to work at a creative agency. Not everyone has a desire to live and die by a projects success. There are much safer ways to make a living. You have to truly give a damn to place your professional reputation on the line each and every day for your client and have confidence in your team to bring dramatic solutions that aren't always the safest or easiest. You may have heard the old mantra "No one ever got fired for hiring IBM." Well, it's time to call bullshit on that. If you aren't pushing the boundaries to continually improve, if what you're pursuing doesn't make you a little scared, this business isn't for you. Marketers who pick the safe choice to protect their job over the success of the company should be fired. Is that a little harsh? Maybe. But that's the shot in the arm that some folks need to finally wake up.

This book is my best attempt at pressing "pause" on the marketing advice saga so we can all take a step back and realize that following the rules isn't as smart as it's cracked up to be. In fact, it might be the worst marketing decision you'll ever make.

Now that we're all acquainted, what should you expect to see in the pages to follow? At a high level, *F*** Your Formula* is a literary cocktail of industry criticism, cautionary tales, and inspiring stories with a golden thread that prods you to push yourself past imaginary guardrails. In the first chapter, we'll identify four psychological biases that stifle independent thinking and tie them back to marketing. After all, if you want to liberate yourself from rigid thinking (and the people who promote it) you have to understand *why* you fall for it in the first place. In chapter two, we'll explore the inherent contradictions in marketing formulas and why you might want to consider blocking those gurus on social media. It might be a tough pill to swallow, but we added some sugar to make the medicine go down easier.

Chapter three explains the worst part about best practices, namely that they don't make you "the best"—they drag you into the middle. Chapter four is about shiny objects, why we love them, and why most of them don't fit. Chapter five addresses risk (or lack thereof) and how risk relates to throwing out your rulebook. In chapter six, we'll outline six mental exercises to foster lateral thinking (yes, we realize the irony of using a formula to break a formula). Lastly, we'll conclude with a simple message: There's a better way. Always. The rules are meant to be broken, bub.

If you're ready to question the so-called experts, think for yourself, and get a good chuckle at the expense of some corny influencers, stay tuned. We've got lots to talk about.

CHAPTER 1

Why Are We Suckers For Formulas?

Business leaders love to follow formulas, understandably so. In a chaotic, unpredictable market, decision-makers desperately want some guiding light. For all the talk of disrupting the status quo, many don't have the stomach for zigging when everyone else zags. They want to follow a formula.

Formulas are one of the most ubiquitous aspects of business, and there is no shortage of them in other fields. Quality improvement specialists are fond of Six Sigma. Actors gravitate to "method" or "Stanislavski's system." Major League Baseball coaches spend hours analysing sabermetrics like wins above replacement.

And then there's the marketing field, where formulas are omnipresent. Marketers throughout the ages have followed and sworn by them. While formulas appear to make life easier on surface level, they're the source of a big problem: they stifle independent thinking—perhaps the most vital tool any marketer can possess.

If we want to liberate ourselves from the flood of marketing formulas (and the gurus that peddle them) that stifle our independent thinking, we first need to understand *why* we fall for them in the first place. After all, we don't consciously decide to become automatons who blindly obey rules from strangers. Over the past 20 years of sitting in meetings, engaging with clients, and taking some hard looks in the mirror, we've noticed four biases that prime marketers for conformity. Here they are.

Survivorship Bias:
If it worked for them, it can work for anybody!

A few years ago at an event for entrepreneurs in St. Louis, my colleagues and I took our seats to listen to a highly anticipated keynote speech from a former rugby coach-turned-motivational speaker (who shall remain nameless). I heard rumors that this guy was getting paid $50,000 to give his speech. Naturally my expectations were high. As I sat on the edge of my seat waiting to hear this big-shot's secret sauce, my hopes were quickly dashed. His story went something like this: the team's plane crashed high up in an icy mountain range—nobody knew where they were; nobody was dressed for the snow and wind; nobody was coming to get them. So, the coach just started walking through the damn mountain range. By a stroke of luck, he eventually reached civilization in the nick of time.

Then came his Big Idea:

"I just kept telling myself, *keep going*. Put one foot in front of the other and keep going. That's my message to you."

As I walked despondently out of the event, I couldn't help but think: *who the f!!ck gave this guy 50 grand to tell us to "keep going?"* Wasteful spending aside, the speech was a textbook example of the "survivorship bias:" our tendency to give preferential treatment to anybody who has tasted success, no matter how outrageous, dangerous, or stupid their means of achieving it. Let's get real: if one hundred people crashed in the middle of a freezing mountain range without adequate food or clothing, how many of them would survive by just "putting one foot in front of the other?" Somewhere in the zero range, right? And yet, the survivorship bias gave that speaker the chutzpah to tell a room full of hopeful entrepreneurs just that.

Since that disappointing experience, I've noticed parallels in the marketing industry. It seems like every hour, a new marketing "influencer" broadcasts their highlight reel to the world with click bait titles like "How to increase your Instagram followers by 7x in 30 days" (that's a real headline, by the way.) They might be slimy snake-oil salespeople, but they have a keen understanding of human psychology. They know up-and-comers are *starving* for solutions served on silver platters, a promise that someone has finally found the secret—and it works all the time.

This begs the question: Why do people fall for the survivorship bias? Perhaps a better question is: Why aren't marketers more skeptical about copying and pasting someone else's strategy? At the risk of sounding harsh, many marketers are flat out lazy. After all, why would you do the hard work of digging to find an answer when somebody else already found the answer—and all you have to do is fork up some cash to get it?

If we want to know why some marketing campaigns are hits, it might seem like common sense to dissect the successful campaigns, identify their attributes, and replicate them. But what that strategy fails to reveal is that if we also dissected campaigns that were catastrophic failures, many of them would likely share the same attributes as the successful ones. In other words, we correlate certain marketing tactics with success when they're equally correlated with failure.

If you pick up a magazine in the check-out line at the grocery store, scroll through your newsfeed, or tune into a daytime TV news show, you're almost guaranteed to hear about a weight loss success story. Does this narrative sound familiar: Somebody struggled with their weight for years until they stumbled upon a new, miraculous diet or exercise program that melted away pounds of fat—but it's not just *any* diet or exercise program. It has a twist, something we haven't heard of, but seems plausible. Like detox, keto, paleo, or all grapefruit all the time! It's usually backed by science, endorsed by doctors or an irritatingly energetic fitness guru. And if it worked for them, it can work for us too, right?

There's a few reasons why the media (and upright mammals) never get tired of weight loss success stories. Traced to their roots, these stories almost always come back to the survivorship bias. Common sense tells us that if we want to *see* success, we must *study* success. If we want to lose 15 pounds and fit into that charming

Speedo with the bedazzled tiger head on the crotch, it would seem logical to replicate the habits of the person who lost 100. However, there's a fundamental flaw of the survivorship bias: It fails to take into account the nuances that constitute success.

Weight loss is not a one-size-fits-all process. Some people require heavy doses of carbs while others need to cut them out altogether. Some people lose weight by running while others have better luck with resistance training. It's related to your personal DNA, for crying out loud! I'm no personal trainer—although I played one on "St. Elsewhere" for three seasons—but I imagine you get the point here. Achieving health goals is less of a standardized formulaic math problem than it is an art project requiring us to account for a multitude of variables.

Let's tie this back to marketing. Every brand or organization has its own ethos. Like a fingerprint, its audience and circumstances are one of a kind. If someone who built an app was able to drive a million downloads through a specific marketing strategy, that has no bearing whatsoever on a brand that's trying to sell diapers. I'm mystified when I attend marketing conferences and I see attendees scrambling to take notes from a keynote speaker who hasn't had a minute of experience in the individual attendees' industries. No matter how impressive that speaker's resume is, the notion that their strategy is replicable, regardless of the situation, is horse shit.

You can find hundreds of marketers who won't hesitate to appease clients by saying, "Yes, you're 100% right—I also saw that article in Forbes/watched that Ted Talk/listened to that podcast, and I think we can get you the same results."

I would not be one of those marketers.

Sure, there's some likelihood that studying others' success can work in your favor. But there's no guarantee. So, on the off chance that the plan would crash and burn while wasting a tremendous amount of time and resources, I'll pass.

The irony is that we all want to share our success stories—it makes us look good and it can feel rewarding to show others how we got there. We say, "Hey, I did XYZ and it worked, so I think you should try it, too." But when the rubber meets the road, there are so many variables at stake that the likelihood of replicating the results is about as feasible as Kanye West demonstrating humility.

Conformity:
Just follow the rules and nobody gets hurt.

Back in the 1970s, the tech community adopted the catch phrase, "Nobody ever got fired for choosing IBM." At the time, IBM was setting the industry standard in tech by introducing the PC. They also had a solid track record with reliable mainframes and workhorse office products
like the Selectric typewriter. As a result, the corporation gained a reputation for being the only safe bet to solve problems in the business world. If an employee was tasked with finding the best piece of software or the best consultants for a certain project, the

default was always IBM. Why? To shield them from repercussions—if the project went into the shitter, it was IBM's fault, not yours.

Fast forward X years and I got my own taste of the nobody-gets-fired-for-choosing IBM phenomenon, and ultimately realized why it's so tempting to conform to authority.

I was a young consultant, subcontracting through Deloitte for the Kinko's-FedEx merger. I was thrilled to be involved on the project, but I could sense my business partner, Will, and I hadn't gained the full trust of FedEx's leadership. So, one day I approached a senior FedEx manager.

"I don't understand," I said. "Will and I have been doing enough work to displace six Deloitte consultants, but we still have to subcontract through Deloitte to get paid. Why don't you just pay us directly?"

"You're exactly right," he told me. "You and Will kick ass. But you have to understand, Brian: if I go to my board and say, 'Hey, I'm going to hire Deloitte to solve this problem,' they'll sign off in a heartbeat. But if I go to the board and vouch for you and Will, I'm putting my ass on the line. If Deloitte fl!cks up, how was I supposed to know? Deloitte solves everyone's problems. But if you guys have one slip-up, you and I are both out of a job."

After he explained the situation in those terms, I thought, "Shit, *now* I get it."

For millions of professionals, especially marketing executives, surviving is a matter of keeping your head down: Be a cog in the wheel, don't put your ass on the line. We're so preoccupied with conforming to the status quo that we rarely, if ever, look outside our bubbles for a new perspective. But on the flip side, achieving anything worth a damn, whether in marketing or anything else, requires us to rock the boat.

Instead of "Nobody gets fired for choosing IBM," I want to start a new catch phrase for marketers: "You **will** definitely get fired for blindly following Gary Vee, **AdWeek** or [insert your favorite influencer here.]" Challenging conformity is risky business, but staying inside of your comfort zone forever entails risks of its own.

I've had the unique horror of attending the shitshow that is South By Southwest—which contains the highest per-capita concentration of bullshit formulas in the world. In 2014, I flew down to Austin for the conference optimistic I'd be exposed to some new ideas that would challenge my thinking about marketing and digital media. Alas, I was sorely disappointed. I made my way up to the "bloggers' lounge" (typing that made me cringe) packed with what I call the "Social Media Douchebag Society" or swarms of bloggers who had fallen in love with their own voices, all convinced that they had the media landscape figured out. For a group that took pride in its curiosity and open-mindedness, I found the conversations startlingly incestuous, almost like a group of middle schoolers gossiping in the cafeteria about Facebook and Twitter.

Don't get me wrong, these were all friendly, well-meaning people, some of whom I consider friends. But from the conversations I had, many of them had not demonstrated any effort to look outside of their own self-important bubbles to back up the claims they were propagating—and I know South by Southwest isn't the only place where this was happening.

Time and time again throughout my career, I've met with leaders who shy away from creative risks, or even new ideas, because they're deathly afraid that behaving in a disruptive manner will compromise their organization's reputation and relationships that have paved their path to success. Accordingly, they'd rather stay the course and do block-and-tackle work rather than striking on an opportunity while the iron is hot. Essentially they stick to the adage that "no one ever got fired for hiring IBM."

Human beings are inherently tribal. We tend to surround ourselves with people who look like us, talk like us, and think like us. We seek comfort in people and situations that mirror our world-view and the biggest offenders are the ones who go out of their way to tell you ad nauseum about their open-mindedness. We trust the crowd because it's a collection of knowledge. As the saying goes, *fifty million Frenchmen can't be wrong*.

Being accepted in the tribe—and staying in the tribe—have been essential behaviors needed to sustain our survival for millions of years. But business has outgrown our massively massive brains, and our fear of becoming the outlier has trickled into brainstorms and meeting rooms where dissenters won't speak out against defunct formulas out of fear of being rejected by the tribe. We don't want to risk social (or business) alienation by challenging the crowd—even when we know the crowd pretty much sucks.

People who conform to the status quo often have a reputation for being dumb or lazy. Truthfully, though, it's fear that fuels confor-mity. We don't break away from our job and start something we've always wanted to start because we're afraid to fail. We don't challenge stale ideas because we're afraid our idea will get raked across the coals or that HR will show up with a box and a security guard to escort us out of the building. History, however, is defined by the individuals who refused to give into the system and ultimately solved a problem by disrupting the norm and doing things differently.

Some people say conformity is the safe choice. I'd argue that it's deadly...and really boring.

Confirmation Bias:
When you're a hammer, everything looks like a nail.

As a father, I find myself wanting to encourage my kids to try all sorts of new sports and activities. But as I talk to other parents about that, it's becoming more and more clear that kids tend to gravitate only towards the activities that come naturally to them. Maybe you've noticed this yourself: you ask a kid, "Why don't you try basketball?" And they say something along the lines of, "Well, I'm not good at basketball, so I don't play it." Inevitably, this mindset creates herds of kids who only seek out opportunities to specialize in one specific activity at the risk of never achieving their true potential.

You don't have to look far to find a similar confirmation bias in the marketing world. Let's say an entrepreneur is launching a new restaurant. In the past, they've had success with influencer marketing to create buzz around new business. By default, there's a good chance that entrepreneur will head over to Google and type in something like:

- **"How to use influencer marketing to launch a restaurant"** or
- **"Best influencer marketing strategies for restaurants"**

Of course, a more logical way for that entrepreneur to approach the situation would be to ask higher-level questions, such as:

- **"What resonates with my target audience?"** or
- **"What am I taking for granted that might not be true this time around?"**

But the confirmation bias is strong. It nudges us to take mental shortcuts and selectively seek information that assuages our egos instead of challenging them. Even the most respected marketing agencies fall victim to the confirmation bias. For example, an agency that's had some success with Instagram stories is pitching a new client. Since the agency is fond of Instagram stories, they'll find a way to persuade the client to use that tactic rather than seeking out information that might conflict with their preference, but ultimately would better help the client.

We had a name for this strategy during my days when I worked at the sports apparel store, Champs: Our mantra was SWAT (sell what's available today). If somebody came into the store wanting to buy the news Jordans but we didn't have them, we'd try to sell them the Barkleys. Even if that's not what the customer wanted or needed, we had to move those Barkleys, or else the customer would take their business elsewhere.

When you're a hammer, everything looks like a nail. If you're a PR firm, every client needs PR. If you're a graphic designer, every client needs a new logo. You get where I'm going with this. We're primed to interpret situations in terms of our existing beliefs, values, or theories, regardless of the evidence. Why? Because deep down, we're all scared as hell that we're wrong.

Did you know that Fireball Whisky (yes, Canadians are communist and their "whisky" is "e"-free) is one of the most consumed spirits in the US? True indeed. And when you think of a prototypical Fireball consumer, who comes to mind? Maybe a rugged, 20-something-year-old dude with a ginormous Jeep who enjoys country music and dirty jokes? If that sounds accurate to you, you're not alone.

That was my initial assumption when our Elasticity team became Fireball's social media agency of record in 2014, managing their organic and paid content on all platforms. Around that same time, Wheeler Walker Jr. (the country music singing alter-ego of comedian Ben Hoffman) was gaining popularity amongst young men with his vulgar country music albums *Redneck Shit* and *Ol' Wheeler*. I thought I had stumbled upon a gem of an influencer. Walker was on the come-up, and we could hook him up with some Fireball swag to build even more momentum for one of the top-selling liquor brands in the country.

But as it turned out, my perception was somewhat off base.

Our team dug into the data to compare Wheeler's fans with Fireball's, and the correlation wasn't terrible, but not what I had presumed would be a home run. Thus, I swallowed my pride when

I saw the data depicting the median age range of Wheeler's fans was higher than Fireball's and he already was an iffy proposition because the brand managers were somewhat conservative. So I put my hands up and said, "Alright, not a good idea. Back to drinking cheap Scotch and listening to Rick Springfield in my office."

Looking back, it's clear that I was falling victim to the confirmation bias: the instinct to overestimate the value of information that confirms our assumptions or expectations. Like it or not, we all have a tendency to jump to conclusions and form hypotheses, especially if we're emotionally involved in the project. As a result, we cherry pick evidence that validates our cherished assumptions and filter out evidence that challenges them. Mission accomplished!

In both business and life, objectivity is a fleeting commodity—like this insufferable woman I know whose Twitter profile hilariously starts with her being "Interested in kindness." Understanding that our rose-colored glasses distort reality and confronting the fact that our deeply-held beliefs are flawed is no easy task. It is easy, however, to fall in love with our own ideas (or the ideas of our favorite guru), regardless of their validity.

If we learned anything from the election of Donald Trump, it's that the social media echo chamber is definite. We inundate ourselves with people and information that echoes what we believe (or want to believe), and we can't get enough of it. When enough people hear what's perceived as insightful or correct, the chamber gets deeper and harder to escape. Whether it's politics or marketing, we don't have to look far to find acolytes that congregate around their guru of choice who churns out content to assuage their egos.

As nice as it would be to have a quick fix for the confirmation bias, it doesn't exist. The best we can do is to exercise a little humility, always keep a beginner's mindset, treat everything as an experiment—hold our own feet to the fire. Otherwise, we're primed to latch onto any mindless tip, trick, hairstyle or hack that seems legit.

Inertia: *But we've always done it that way*

You might have first heard the term "inertia" in a middle school physics class. If you need a refresher, inertia is an object's resistance to any changes in speed or direction. Things in motion tend to stay in motion. But inertia affects people, too—especially those who have steadily made their way up the totem pole throughout their career. As we get older, our thought patterns crystalize. Like cement, our ideas solidify and become harder and harder to break. Our thinking becomes rigid and one-dimensional. Does this mean we're lazy or stupid? Not at all (at least in most cases). In observing colleagues in marketing, both older and younger, it seems like a lot of inertia stems from fear.

When you move up in an agency (or any organization for that matter), you take on more responsibilities. Eventually, there might be dozens or even thousands of people that rely on you for a paycheck that puts food on the table for their families. There's a mortgage to pay and kids to support. These factors tend to make a person overly cautious. The last thing you'll want to do is deviate from what got you to the top of the hill in the first place. With everything on the line, you can't afford to stir up controversy—so you play it safe and ride it out until retirement.

On the other hand, there's usually a room full of young creatives and ambitious account managers who are eager to push the limits: *Let's disrupt all of this boring old shit! Who cares if somebody sues us or calls the cops? Any publicity is better than no publicity!*

And yet, the senior manager resists—they give in to the inertia of the old ways. If the junior copywriter gets in trouble, that's no big deal. After all, they have nothing to lose. But the executive is responsible for their house, their kid's college fund, and maybe the entire organization. So, they suppress anything that threatens what's already been established. Whenever a radical idea bubbles up from underneath, they force it back down like repressed childhood trauma or just some acid reflux.

But there's a tradeoff here.

In creative pursuits like marketing, higher risk yields higher rewards (if you play your cards right). Ironically, we're seeing agencies and brands alike shying away from risk, even though consumers are tired of being fed the same old bullshit. For example, if a brand has been running 30-second TV spots since the 80s, it's going to be incredibly difficult for them to experiment with a new platform like TikTok, even if they have evidence that their target audience wants them there.

Look, I get it: you won't get hit by a bus if you never go outside. But outside is where all the fun is.

"Aaron, let me tell you why you couldn't be more wrong."

I remember those words like it was yesterday—the response I received from my supervisor, an executive at a respected global communications firm which shall remain nameless. The year was 2007 and our team was tasked with promoting economic development in a large metro region. The communications landscape was undergoing a seismic shift—we *had* to dramatically change our approach towards managing reputation and building brands—and I suggested we approach the task through the prism of how human beings were beginning to find most of their information at the time as well as today: through search engines.

We had gone to lunch to discuss the client and the conversation began with a simple question.

"What do you think we should be doing for the client?" he asked.

"Well, I think we need to focus on search," I responded. "We need to create an online vehicle or platform that frames and articulates the live, work, and play value proposition of the region and then we need to invest in organic and paid search to ensure the right eyeballs are on it."

Then he hit me the warmly memorable, "Let me tell you why you couldn't be more wrong." His solution?

"We need to be in the pages of *The Wall Street Journal, The New York Times* and *USA Today.*"

Such fresh thinking for 1977! Let's get one or two media placements in top tier outlets to assuage everyone's egos—never mind if it was the in the client's best interest.

I stood my ground despite realizing this old, excessively angry man wouldn't recognize progress if it bit him in the ass with Gary Busey's choppers. But alas, my plea—and this was the first of many—went nowhere. We were simply tarred, feathered, forced back into the salt mines, and a variety of other euphemisms essentially saying we went back to wasting the client's valuable marketing dollars.

Meanwhile, I started plotting my exit.

Whether you call this inertia, stagnation, fear or complacency, it's one of the most dangerous traps any marketer can fall into. When we get too comfortable and only rely on what worked in back in the day, we produce mediocre work. We check a box. We tread water. And ironically, many of the narrow-minded people affected by inertia, including the man in my story (who thankfully retired 12 years too late), sit atop the totem poles at brands and agencies alike.

Instead of seeking what's in the best interest of an audience or a brand in an effort to truly create a return on an investment in marketing communications, inertia cajoles us into doing what's familiar. Left unchecked, familiarity can breed failure.

–|–

These biases usually get the most attention when they're applied to economics or sociology. But as you can see, marketers can be especially vulnerable to them. Maybe you've even experienced them in your own career. Fortunately, becoming aware of these biases is the first step to loosening their grip.

So what?

1. The survivorship bias tempts us to follow anybody who has tasted success, regardless of how outrageous, dangerous, or stupid their means of achieving it were.

2. Conforming is often just as dangerous as breaking the rules.

3. Our brains are primed to cherry pick information that confirms our beliefs instead of challenging them.

4. The longer we remain entrenched in certain strategy or belief, the harder it becomes to break free from it.

CHAPTER 2

The Super Secret Success Recipe (Hint: It Doesn't Exist)

Bernie Taupin, Elton John's songwriting partner, was cruising down the highway back to his hometown in rural England when the words came to him:

> *She packed my bags last night, pre-flight*
> *Zero hour: 9 a.m.*
> *And I'm gonna be high as a kite by then*
> *I miss the Earth so much, I miss my wife*
> *It's lonely out in space*
> *On such a timeless flight*

Taupin reached into his glove compartment in search of something, anything to capture those words. But the glove box was empty. No pen. No pad. No recorder. The then-22-year-old Taupin, veins surging with adrenaline, resorted to his last and only solution: he repeated those 40 words over and over aloud to himself for hours until he arrived at his parents' house. When his mom and dad approached his car to greet him, he sprinted past them to find the nearest pad and pen.

Those 40 words would become the opening stanza of "Rocket Man," which soared to the top of the charts upon release and now sits among *Rolling Stone's* 500 greatest songs of all time. But you're probably asking yourself, "What the hell does this have to do with marketing?"

Hear us out.

There's a myth that successful marketing can be treated like a math problem that can only be solved by an elite ruling class of clear-framed-glasses-wearing *Forbes* contributors in L.A. or New York—as if there's a vending machine of ideas that requires a secret password. But as the Taupin story illustrates, even the most talented people on the planet, marketers included, don't rely on formulas to produce great work (and if they did, they certainly wouldn't be plastering it all over their books, keynote speeches, and social media accounts.)

Truthfully, there is no creative director, no guru, no whiz kid who can shift a paradigm on demand. That's because breakthrough ideas have little to do with secret recipes and everything to do with patience, relaxation, random thoughts, a news story flashing across a screen, or just dumb luck. Technology will give us self-driving cars. Robotics will make factory workers obsolete. But computers will never replace artists, writers, and entrepreneurs.

Whether it's coming up with the lyrics to a perennial hit or envisioning your brand's new tagline, there's virtually no limit to what the human mind can produce. You have more than 100 trillion synapses in your brain which give you access to an infinite pool of ideas. But to think that you or your guru of choice can systematize those synapses to work on-demand is a recipe for frustration.

If There Was a Secret Sauce, It Wouldn't Be For Sale

In March 2016, a contributor at a respected global media outlet hit "publish" on an article that made waves on social media with the boisterous headline "10 Marketing Secrets That Can Make Anything Go Viral." Skeptical, but admittedly curious, I bit on the clickbait.

Less than two paragraphs into the article, the author blatantly admitted that "there is no specific formula to make something go viral."

Then why the hell waste your time (and everybody else's) by writing this pile of crap? I thought to myself.

Nevertheless, the contributor still had plenty of white space to fill and proceeded to list ten relatively worthless "secrets" which were purportedly the ingredients for making a product or business to go viral. This included never-before-seen insights such as "be authentic," "have a clear voice," and most important of all, "be great."

Five minutes spent that I'll never get back.

I don't mean to single this person out. I'm sure they are well-meaning and bright. As most of us know full well, there are thousands of culprits when it comes to peddling similar promises about marketing success. But at the heart of these promises is a paradox: If some self-proclaimed, omniscient marketing "expert" or "guru" or "karate bacon enthusiast" really **did** possess some secret that could propel a brand to the top of everyone's minds, wouldn't it be idiotic for them to write articles, publish books and give talks in which they give it all away?

The irony in the notion that someone tells you they have the key, and they're happy to give it away if you simply click their dubious headlines, or worse, cough up money to watch them speak, should immediately trigger your bullshit detector. It's sort of like when someone comes up to you and says, "Dude, you know I'd never lie to you"—as the guy who ran my kid's hockey club used to say to me each time I asked him a substantive question—well that's your first clue to knowing that person is full of shit and is probably lying to you.

If there's one thing I've learned in 832 years of professional failure...I mean...during my time as a semi-professional professional, it's that there are no marketing "truths." There are just a conglomeration of opinions from individual marketers who rely on their intuition to speculate about how their ideas will play out in the real world. And opinions are like assholes—everyone's got one and they all stink. So if I'm being honest, this book itself is just another opinion amongst many. Whether you take it as gospel or tear it to shreds is up to you. Either way, I'll be the first to admit I don't have it all figured out, except when it comes to mustaches, bacon, beer, the Muppets, Mr. T and mullets.

Only one thing is certain: If I had that "cheat code," I'd keep it under wraps instead of broadcasting it to the world (like the books next to this one might).

When David Ogilvy published *Confessions of an Advertising Man* in 1963, it instantly became required reading for anybody hoping to break into the industry. Among the eleven chapters are "How to Build Great Campaigns,""How to Write Potent Copy," and "How to Rise to the Top of the Tree." It sold 5,000 copies within its first month in print, and today there are well over one million copies of *Confessions* collecting dust on bookshelves around the world.

To promote his book, Ogilvy ran a series of ads with headlines such as "Every secret but one is in this book" and "How to create financial advertising that sells." At the time, this was one of the first books about advertising to ever be published, and the fact that it was penned by the most sought after ad man in the world made it even more compelling.

Ogilvy's colleagues and coworkers were quick to judge him: *Are you insane?! Why would you give away all your secrets?!* But Ogilvy understood two things:

- Anybody that tried to replicate what his agency had already done would simply come off as a phony, a copycat.
- And more importantly, he knew his book would position him as the expert.

Brand managers weren't going to put in the work to learn how to write Ogilvy-level copy—they'd simply come knock on his door to have him do it.

In other words, he wasn't giving away the secrets—Ogilvy knew damn well that there were no secrets. He was, however, really good at making people *feel like* he was giving away the secrets.

Sounds familiar, right?

Now, we see the same scenario play out every day. The only differences are that marketers are selling their "secrets" online, and there's way more than just one guy doing it. All it takes is a quick Google search to confirm this: *How to write headlines*. As I write this, there are 134 million results for that query and counting. Of course, the same applies for "how to go viral" or "how to get more subscribers." But if we're being honest, are the people who publish this content doing so because they found a secret and now decided to share it with you (whether for free or for a fee) out of the kindness of their hearts? Not by a long shot. Like Ogilvy did in the 60s, they're helping themselves, not you. In fact, the real secret here might be "How to make money off of getting people to think you're giving them the magic beans." No returns, all sales final.

Here's the bottom line: If you can access these tips, tricks, and instructions, so can anybody else with an internet connection. Not so secret anymore, eh?

Information Obesity

The late journalist A.J. Liebling once said that freedom of the press is only guaranteed to those who own one. This may have been true during his tenure as a prodigious correspondent for *The New Yorker* in the mid-1900s, but our 21st-century media landscape has now caught up with Liebling's witty remark.

Take a moment to consider the power of the pre-internet media: writers, editors, and producers at the various publications served as the gatekeepers of information, meaning they controlled what and how much news or entertainment their audiences received. Companies and individuals alike were dependent on these publications for coverage. What's more, these media outlets had a finite amount of space to fill for their daily or weekly issues. Bottom line: If they decided to give you the time of day, they were doing you a huge favor. You could think of the media back then as a buyer's market—which is why publishers were gazillionaires back in the day. Today's media landscape is topsy-turvy. The internet has turned the media into a seller's market.

As blogging and self-publishing gained momentum in the early 2000s, former *Financial Times* tech reporter and ambrosia-fiend Tom Foremski was one of the first to predict that brands and individuals alike would all become self-publishers in order to build their online reputations. Furthermore, he recognized that they would have to "feed the beast" by publishing insane amounts of content, leading them to spout off countless ideas, some viable, many of them ludicrous.

The utopian vision of self-publishing in the digital age was that the best ideas would rise to the top. But as we can see, particularly in the marketing industry, the glut of information that we're inundated with has left audiences dazed and confused. In the old days, a few publications such as *Advertising Age* were the sole voices in the industry. With less people shoving their opinions in your face, it was easier to think independently. Today, however, there are millions of digital voices yelling at us from every direction, telling us how to run campaigns, how to steal people's attention, and how to drive results. Surely, out of this pile of solutions, one of them must be worthwhile, right? And thus we go down the rabbit hole, eating ourselves, metaphorically, into information obesity.

In terms of content, there is no correlation between quantity and quality. In fact, there might even be a negative correlation. As my former client would put it, "There's no need to boil the ocean." As tempting as it is to believe that we can find the needle in the haystack, it's incumbent upon us, as individuals, to craft our own solution that fits our culture, our audience, and our brand. Rather than complicitly feeding the beast, we would do well to go on an information diet.

In one of Neal Brennan's standup comedy routines, he has a bit about the porn industry that I realized was just as relevant to the marketing industry. Hear me out.

"If you work in porn, I don't know if you and your coworkers know this, but *we have enough porn.* You don't have to keep making it. We appreciate your service, but you can shut it down."

The first time I heard this, my mind went straight to, *Hey marketing gurus, we have enough marketing "secrets." There are more than we can ever go through. For the love of God, give it a rest.*

Despite the fact that we're drowning in content put out by self-promotional marketers, we can't seem to get enough of it. Every day, thousands of marketing books are sold, millions of blog posts are shared, and videos rack up millions of views. Audiences full of marketers eagerly wait to hear from experts with their unique, proven formula.

Inevitably, consumers don't get the immediate results that were promised, so they toss it into the pile of useless content and move on to the next book, the next blog post, and the next video in hopes that *this is the one.* It's a variation of FOMO (fear of missing out.) The ceaseless chatter coming at us from all directions prompts us to think, "Oh my God, what if the answer was in that book over there or this Ted Talk over here?" Accordingly, we dig a smattering of shallow holes without ever committing to a single strategy, much less put in the work to develop our own unique strategy. The answer must be here somewhere—I just need to cover every base.

Compulsive information consumption is also akin to compulsive gambling: the next scratch-off ticket will be a winner, the next hand of blackjack will go in your favor; you keep doubling down in hopes that one bet will recoup all the money you squandered, but deep down you know it's a futile habit. The same goes for marketers who can't get enough content. They double down on their efforts to find "the answer," often spending money in the process, when nobody can truly give them the answer.

I was recently talking to the founder of a successful swimwear brand, when this topic of information obesity came up. She hit the nail on the head: "I don't have time for any conferences, seminars, or any of that stuff," she said. "I'm building a brand. The most successful entrepreneurs are the ones who aren't wasting their time and money to ask someone else for the answers, they're learning the answers by *doing*."

I couldn't have said it better myself. The best marketers aren't necessarily the ones with sell-out speaking gigs or flashy social media profiles—the best marketers are the ones you've never heard of, the ones that put in the f!!cking work.

The Shoe That Fits One Person Pinches the Other

If you've ever sat down with an advisor in the financial services industry, chances are they've shown you a bunch of fancy charts that illustrate their past success. It's a powerful persuasion technique, considering how hard it is to argue against data showing hockey stick growth. However, in every contract, advisors are required by law to include a disclosure that says "past performance is not indicative of future results." This ensures that a client can't sue their advisor if their portfolio tanks, even if the advisor was acting in the client's best interest all along.

Don't get me wrong: I'm not saying we shouldn't trust financial advisors—after all, they're professionals with centuries of data to guide their decisions. But at the end of the day, someone's financial wellbeing is riding on a series of educated guesses, which is why that disclaimer must exist to keep everyone honest.

If you look closely at the mouse type on a financial advisor's bio, it says "NO Bank Guarantee" and "You MAY Lose Value." Gulp. There's no sure thing, and that's certainly evident in creative arts. The great screenwriter William Goldman famously said of predicting a hit movie "Nobody knows anything. Not one person in the entire motion picture field knows for a certainty what's going to work. Every time out it's a guess and, if you're lucky, an educated one."

The Wild West of marketing, as we all know, is far less regulated than financial services. Agencies and consultants will do just about anything to get new business in the door, and they're certainly not required by law to end all of their pitches and case studies with a disclaimer that says, "past performance is not indicative of future results."

But should they?

It's hard to imagine a bigger buzzkill after a potential client is riding the high of an agency's compelling work samples and a new campaign concept. But who's to say those results can be replicated or if that concept will resonate with a different audience? Making an informed decision grounded in data and insights is one thing, but salivating over a strategy simply because it worked wonders for a previous client or because it was cooked up by a prestigious creative director is a recipe for frustration and disaster. As the famous historian Arnold Toynbee wrote, "No tool is omnicompetent. There is no such thing as a master-key that will unlock all doors."

Rather than admitting that marketing is a semi-controlled crapshoot, there are armies of online pundits who promise their potential customers that they can drive an unprecedented number of traffic to their site overnight or get them 100,000 Instagram subscribers in 30 days. Let's say they did achieve those numbers in the past; that doesn't mean the strategy can or should be copied and pasted over and over. For example, a young marketer who *Business Insider* dubbed a "social media savant" became an overnight celebrity after he orchestrated a stunt where he buried hundreds of dildos on beaches in Los Angeles. As offensive or awesome as that sounds (depending on your level of tolerance), it worked for one extraordinarily shameless client. The stunt garnered tons of earned media coverage with brand pull-through. But imagine an established, professional brand with a loyal following trying to pull off a similar stunt—they'd get raked across the coals by board members and audiences alike.

So, the next time you read an attention-grabbing success story, you'd do well to remember the same disclaimer your financial advisor gives you: *past performance is not indicative of future results*.

Let's take a moment to talk about an industry that's notoriously boring, bland, and bothersome: banking. If you look at banks today, they've blended together and become commoditized. It's like walking into a botanical garden on a Sunday and seeing some asshole family with quadruplets all dressed in the same outfits. It doesn't matter if you're Bank of America, Citi, Regions Bank or US Bank—none of them are going to put any extra money into your savings account. As a result, the banks that have endeavored to break through the clutter and deviate from the stale marketing formulas that every other damn bank has relied on for decades are the ones who have grown and succeeded beyond simply having a large geographical footprint.

One such bank is our former client Capital One, which most recently launched its line of Capital One Cafés to build brand affinity with younger audiences—the same consumers who are often skeptical of large financial institutions. This venture is still young, and their spokesperson has enormous hands which stand out to me in each commercial, but all signs indicate that this refreshing take on banking was a smart path to pursue. Capital One formerly leveraged its annual Mascot Challenge over the years to connect with college students, a project we were fortunate to work on. Rather than drowning students in facts and figures, the Mascot Challenge created a shared language between Capital One and an otherwise elusive audience by giving millions of college students an opportunity to engage and start a conversation. It's simply about getting credit cards into the wallets of young people, nothing more, nothing less.

Rather than simply treading water, Rich Fairbank and Capital One's leadership has always had a unique manner of looking at the banking landscape and blowing it up. They continue to ask how they can target a very specific audience and engage with them by tapping into things they actually care about to break through the clutter. They look at where human culture is going and create a new model for themselves—and it works every time (as does Colt 45 according to my man Billy Dee Williams).

But let's take a step back: Just because a mascot challenge or a hipster banking café works for Capital One does not mean it works for, say, Bic pens, Edible Arrangements, Crocs or any other brand for that matter. Can crossover appeal work when it comes to marketing strategies? Sure, it can. But the landscape is too fluid to be treated as an exact science and brands really thrive on customization, not replication.

But don't just take my word for it. Take it from Saul Alinsky (I love guys named "Saul"), the father of modern community organization and author of the perennial seller on creating real change, *Rules for Radicals*:

"There can be no prescriptions for particular situations because situations rarely recur. Particular combinations exist only in a particular time—even then the variables are in flux. Tactics must be understood as specific applications of principles. To these he applies his imagination, and he relates them tactically to specific situations."

Translation: cut out the copy-and-paste bullshit, because the best practice for you is also the best practice for everyone else.

Don't Be Next, Be First

There's a shit-ton of people who have gotten on a motorcycle and jumped over 50 cars. Name two of them.

If you're like most people, you'll answer, "Evil Kneivel, and uh…."

The world is littered with stunt devils who have replicated Evil Kneivel's memorable motorcycle stunts, but he was always the first to try the craziest tricks, and that's why he's the greatest. Not to mention, he also had a kick-ass name to match his gig. Our brains, amazing as they are, have a finite capacity. That's why we remember firsts: our first kiss, our first car, our first job. It's also why we remember winners. It's far easier to remember who won the Super Bowl last year or who holds the world record in the 100 meter dash than it is to remember the loser or the second-fastest.

Given this pervasive truth, it's startling how many marketers haven't caught on. In Marketing 101, first-year college students learn that differentiating your brand from others is fundamental to the success of any business. However, when the rubber meets the road, even the best marketers are guilty of conforming to trends, best practices, and formulas.

Everyone is doing retargeting! I need to learn that! Everyone is getting media coverage! I need to pitch more reporters!

Does that mean retargeting or PR never works? Of course not. We use both all the time--but only if it's the right tactic for the right client at the right time.

I've always joked that I wanted to put up a bookshelf with all of the best-selling marketing books and then tell our team, "Don't do any of this shit." Why? Because if a book sold 50,000 copies, I know there's at least a few thousand people who are going to do whatever that author told them to do, and I sure as hell don't want to blend in.

If the core of marketing is finding ways to be different, why the f!!ck would you want to execute the same as everybody else? Think about it like soccer: you don't pass to a person, you pass to space. That is, you anticipate where your teammate is going, not where everybody is packed together.

Find the space and go there. If you can be the first one to get there, you win. But if you're the second one there, you lose.

How do you market a city or region? That's the question we asked ourselves in 2015 when the University of Illinois and the Champaign County Economic Development Corporation challenged us to rebrand their community to attract the talent needed to fill critical jobs and continue fostering a culture of innovation moving forward.

The university's top ranked software engineering program prompted dozens of global companies to migrate to Champaign and its neighboring city, Urbana. However, these companies created a demand for even more software engineers than the company could produce (a good problem to have, if there ever was one.)

I'd love to tell you that after talking with the university and key stakeholders, it became clear that we needed to create a brand that was disruptive and balanced the region's reputation for innovation with the vibrant, welcoming community. But my brain just doesn't work that way. However, as we spoke with community leaders to understand the region's value proposition, we quickly discovered that Champaign-Urbana was home to countless innovations: the Web browser, plasma television screens, the MRI machine, the engine behind the iPhone's Siri, a few kickass video games, whipped cream in a can for Christ's sake, and dozens more—all from two relatively small towns in the middle of Illinois farm country.

But few people outside of the region knew all of this originated in little Champaign-Urbana.

We were sitting in a room with—and I kid you not—roughly 30 stakeholders. They were going on and on about the region's list of innovations and I blurted out, "Huh, you should really just tell people 'you're welcome,' as in, 'You busted up your knee? Well, you're welcome for that MRI machine.'"

And out of a visceral reaction, an idea was born around crafting a campaign from the double entendre of "you're welcome:" the aforementioned snarky comment along with the modest and welcoming, "You're welcome to join our community." That became the springboard for a fully-integrated campaign that brought fresh tech talent into town and galvanized the community of Champaign-Urbana—all on a relatively shoestring budget.

We didn't try to recreate Silicon Valley in the heartland of America or make Champaign-Urbana "weird" because Austin, Texas is "weird." (Portland, weird too). We didn't want to make Champaign-Urbana the "next" anything, and neither did the community. Instead, we chipped away until we discovered what made them, well, **them,** and used that as fuel for the fire.

If you want to grow something big, you have to find that kernel of an insight, which every brand (or city) has. Find what's special for you, not what's been special for a hundred others.

-|-

In school, we were taught there's a definitely correct answer for everything. We were taught that there's a precise equation we can run to find a solution. This mindset, however, is profoundly not the case in the working world, especially in a creative industry such as marketing. The big secret is there is no big secret, so let's put all the textbooks and talks on hold so we can snap back to reality.

So What?

1. If anybody *really* had the secret sauce to go viral, magically increase sales, or get you on the front page of *The New York Times*, they wouldn't give it away or sell it— they'd keep it locked up for eternity, like the Coca-Cola recipe.

2. The never-ending flood of marketing advice, tricks, tips, and hacks is proof in itself that none of them are legit. If they were, why keep publishing more?

3. If you find yourself falling for a quick gimmick, remember: The world values customization and first-evers, not copycats and followers.

CHAPTER 3

The Worst Part About Best Practices

Take a trip down memory lane to your high school glory days: Do you remember the most popular fashion trends of that time? Were parachute pants in? Maybe a perm or platform heels? Regardless of the time, fashion trends have always been powerful. They create a mutually agreed-upon set of guidelines—they're like a social GPS that tells us how to fit in. Put simply, you can think of a fashion trend as a best practice.

But there's a flip side to fashion trends.

If high school hallways were flooded with denim jackets and acid washed jeans, everyone might have felt safe because they were fitting in, but there was an unintended consequence—nobody could make a bold statement. Generally speaking, people don't follow fashion trends because they like a particular style, but because *everyone else* supposedly likes a particular style. As a result, millions of people follow along. That is, until a brave iconoclast, fashionista, or whatever you want to call the innovator, invents a new style (or resurrects an old one).

It may seem like a stretch, but high school fashion trends have a lot in common with marketing best practices. How? Because differentiating yourself from the crowd is a near-impossible feat when you limit yourself to what everyone else is doing. Today's audiences are quicker than ever to sniff out a brand that's walking and talking like everybody else. Does this mean that best practices are inherently wrong or that you'll fail if you follow them? Not at all. But just because one best practice is valuable doesn't mean a brand or career should be defined by them.

"Best practices are nothing more than possibilities," says Jay Acunzo, author of **Break the Wheel**. "The real value today lies **not** in obeying those best practices, but vetting them to decide whether or not they make sense for your specific set of circumstances."

Chugging the Content Kool-Aid

In early 2019, an SEO master guru+ninja+hacker+expert who shall not be named published an admittedly intriguing article: "We Analyzed 912 Million Blog Posts. Here's What We Learned About Content Marketing."

The author's website, which touts a technique that "almost guarantees that you get high quality links from every piece of content that you publish," is an SEO bible for brands and marketers alike. He has the classic candid speaking gig pictures, and he's been pimped by all the usual media suspects: *Forbes, Huffpost, Entrepreneur, Social Media Today* and perhaps even *High Times Magazine* and *Tiger Beat.*

Naturally, my curiosity forced me to bite on the headline. After all, I'm always game for new insights, especially if they can help me do better work. But after about two minutes of trying to digest the article, I got a headache. The incessant percentages, charts, and graphs made me feel like I was back in college cramming for a statistics class rather than learning anything meaningful about content marketing. Call me a radical idealist, but I'm pretty sure content marketing should be treated as an art form, with room for nuance and agile thinking. Not with this master ninja guy. In his world, content marketing can be reduced to a cold, sterile math problem.

Here's the anatomy of an optimal blog post, if you follow his "best practice:"

- Write a post between 1,000 and 2,000 words (because they get more backlinks);
- Make the headline 14-17 words long (because those get more social shares);
- Make the headline a question with the words "what" or "why" (those also get more social shares); and
- Make the article a listicle if possible.

Ok, got it. With this newfound secret sauce for savvy content marketing, I was tempted to write a 2,000-word article titled, "Why do marketing gurus still publish really long studies about shortcuts that don't exist?" Since the article didn't mention anything about the substance of the content itself, I was just going to type *lorem ipsum* until the word count hit 2,000, add a bunch of links, and click "publish."

I digress but hopefully you're smelling what I'm cooking here (copyright infringement: Johnson, Dwayne).

All sarcasm aside, this study is a microcosm of the marketing industry's insatiable appetite for best practices. We salivate at the sound of absolutes, generalities, and patterns. *Yay! Less work for me!* But there's a fundamental problem with best practices: If it's the best practice for you, it's also the best practice for everyone else that uses that best practice. How is anybody supposed to make something remarkable, that is worth remarking, by simply copying and pasting the industry standard? That's like trying to get ahead in traffic when everyone's driving down a one-lane road.

Blindly duplicating what's worked in the past (in this case, characteristics of blog posts that get shared on social media and rank well on Google) doesn't elevate us to the top. Rather, it drags us all into the middle—into eternal averagedom with the NBA's New York Knicks and comic Sinbad. And now, thanks to the proliferation of data trend pieces, it has never been easier to be average. As former Googler Jay Acunzo remarked, the author should've titled his study "We Analyzed 912 Million Blog Posts. *Here's How to Create Perfectly Forgettable Content Marketing.*"

I did a Command+F search for "quality" within his article. Nothing. I also searched for "resonate," "value," and "engage"—characteristics that can't be measured, but are the vital signs of marketing content in any form. Nada, zilch, zero. It felt like I was in a kitchen with a bunch of fancy equipment and no food. It's safe to say the author (and other like-minded automatons) has it all backwards. They obsess over generating leads instead of creating something worth leading people towards. In this worldview, linking to other websites is more important than linking with the emotions of a human being.

And yet, many marketers still roll their eyes at consumers who say they're drowning in boring, irrelevant, needlessly long content.

So, go ahead and write that 1,000 to 2,000-word listicle with a long title that contains a question mark—if that's exactly what it takes to convey your unique message to your unique audience in your unique set of circumstances. Unless your audience hates long-form content, then you might want to write something short and punchy. Unless your audience is obsessed with long-form storytelling, in which case you might want to write a 3,000-word article. Unless your audience hates blogs more than anything, in which case you might want to try videos, podcasts, sandwich boards, or wacky waving inflatable arm flailing tube men.

So, yeah: 1,000 – 2,000-word listicles with long titles that contain question marks. That's it.

At the end of his article, the author posed the question: "What's your #1 takeaway lesson from this study? … Leave a comment right now."

Here's my takeaway: What the hell happened to throwing out the rulebook and just creating kick-ass content?

The Best, Best Practices Are the Ones You Haven't Heard Of

When entrepreneurs come up with new, breakthrough ideas, many have the tendency to immediately think: I'm going to patent this. So, they go to a patent attorney, but they don't like what they hear. The entrepreneur quickly learns that it will cost them as much as twenty grand to secure the patent. Worse still, somebody overseas can rip off your idea since the patent is only valid in the U.S. And that's not even safe. Even in the U.S., somebody can analyze your idea, make one tiny tweak, and all of a sudden they've circumvented any patent violations. Unless you have a six figure legal budget to protect yourself from patent infringement, you're shit out of luck.

So, what's a cash-strapped entrepreneur to do?

Over the past decade of advising startups, the best piece of advice for startups without an army of silk-stalking lawyers as their entourage I've come across is this: **The best protection for your company is to build brand loyalty and stay ahead of the curve.** In other words, don't worry about protecting a patent—by the time everyone rips off your idea, you should be ready to launch a new version or a new product or created a new category altogether. As long as you are looking forward at the next thing, it won't matter if there's a herd of copycats on your heels trying to replicate what you did last year.

Now, let's tie this back to the best practices dilemma.

Everyone is competing for audiences' attention. In order to stay top of mind, marketers are seeking out the best practices to do just that. By the time a specific strategy or tactic gets out into the mainstream media, it has already run its course. Meanwhile, the marketers that are genuinely hungry (like the innovative entrepreneurs) are working relentlessly to challenge the best practices of old so they can stay ahead of the game. They are already looking at the next goalpost while everyone else is trying to figure out how to replicate what they just did.

By the time someone learns a best practice, be it in a book, a blog post, or anywhere else, it's old news. You're studying something that worked yesterday, but may not work when you apply it tomorrow. While the followers are trying to pin down the best practice, a select few are free to think ahead because they know that there's always a better way, even if they haven't discovered it yet.

In other words, the best, best practices are the ones nobody knows about, and the future belongs to marketers that can find them first. But here's the caveat: Nobody can help you do that but yourself (or at least not another marketer that's trying to make a buck off of syndicating their content).

Soft Cookies for the Win

Back in 1977, a 21-year-old woman named Debbi Fields applied for a loan to open up a cookie store in Palo Alto, California. Debbi made a mean cookie, but there was one problem: Her cookies were soft. *But wait*, you say, *soft cookies rule!* Yes, you're 100 percent correct, but unfortunately banks didn't share the same taste back then. Accordingly, Debbi Fields' loan applications were rejected by numerous bankers.

"America likes crispy cookies, not soft, chewy cookies like you make," one asshole lender said.

While the rest of America was obsessed with Chips Ahoy!, Debbi finally got her shot at introducing her strangely soft cookies to the world when she got a loan (with 21% interest). Once people got a taste, they never looked back. Now, more than four decades after she secured her loan, Mrs. Fields Original Cookies is one of the largest retailers of baked goods in the world, employing 4,000 people in 300 locations.

Can I get a hell yeah (copyright infringement: Austin, Steve)?

Now, we have to ask ourselves: Did Debbi Fields carve out a name for herself by pledging allegiance to a set of standards that worked for a bunch of other bakeries? Hell no. When she was trying to convince the bankers that people would like soft cookies, she probably heard something along the lines of, "If people didn't enjoy cookies that crunch, they would have stopped eating them by now."

But that's a logical fallacy. The reality is that people simply **didn't know** they'd fall in love with crunchy cookies until someone introduced them. But if Debbi would have played it safe, her business would have been nothing more than a commodity.

Do you remember this really thin dude who wore black mock turtlenecks and developed modestly popular piece of technology called the iPhone? Yeah, well, Steve Jobs was friggin' brilliant at telling us what we wanted before we knew we wanted it.

It's tempting to think that best practices earn their status because they produce the best results or because they've been around for long periods of time. Both of those assumptions are incorrect. A best practice rises to prominence because it worked in a particular set of circumstances (think Chips Ahoy!). Instead of deviating from that practice, people invest more time and money into it, thus reinforcing the cycle. Meanwhile, a better idea is hanging out there, untouched (like maybe in 2005 we could've used one singular device to talk to and electronic message others through, use as a calculator or flashlight, pay bills on, search the web on).

Making crunchy cookies wasn't the "best practice" because those were the best cookies. It was the best practice because giant corporations were making millions of dollars off of them. That's why so many others wanted to get a piece of the action. However, contrary to what we've all been told, best practices aren't a recipe for growth, innovation is. Best practices can often **inhibit** growth. Why? Because they perpetuate taking the path of least resistance instead of prodding us to push the envelope.

All of this isn't to say you should try to convert people back to crunchy cookies or use flip phones for the sake of being different—although a crunchy cookie inside of a soft cookie, now *that* might be something. But you can keep your flip phones.

Take Notes from George Costanza

In the season five finale of *Seinfeld*, "The Opposite," George comes to grips with an existential crisis: Despite trying his best to live his best life, his life has been in the shitter for 30+ years. After a day of moping around at the beach, George vents his frustration to Jerry and Elaine.

"Why did it all turn out like this for me? I had so much promise. It all became very clear to me sitting out there today, that every decision I've ever made in my entire life has been wrong. Every instinct I have…something to wear, something to eat, it's all been wrong."

George jokes that ordering chicken salad on rye instead of his usual tuna on toast might bring him a turn of luck. But then, Jerry stumbles upon a big idea.

"If every instinct you have is wrong, **then the opposite would have to be right.**"

In George's case, doing the opposite meant being honest, being upfront with women, and having patience. No wonder his life gets better—the opposite of George is a good person. The absurdity is totally obvious, yet hilarious.

So, what can George Costanza's epiphany teach us about marketing? You might see the analogy between his frustration with life and marketers' frustrations with best practices. If you're doing everything you're supposed to, following all the rules to a T, and trusting what the experts say, how can you still be stagnant? I don't have the answer to that, just like George and his friends didn't have the answer for why his life sucked. But that's not the point. The point is that in some cases, a brilliant way to escape inertia and stagnation is to simply think or do the opposite: Is your digital advertising ROI flatlining? Why not double down on PR or experiential? Look at the cannabis industry. For years you've heard about "headshops" but have you heard of the new classy, haute couture shop on Madison Ave.? When they zig, you zag.

We saw a perfect example of this with the launch of Liquid Death: the tech bro-branded canned water. In an industry saturated with crisp, clean branding, fresh streams, and clear plastic packaging, Liquid Death did a 180 by packaging water in metal tall boys and creating cartoons of people getting their heads chopped off and a video of an actress waterboarding a guy in a suit.

"For years, a bunch of marketing f!!ck boys have tricked you into thinking that water is just some girly drink for yoga moms," she says.

Their tagline? *Murder your thirst*.

The creators of Liquid Death weren't sitting around a conference table thinking, "Ok, here's the industry standard for water, how can we compete with that?" Instead, they said, "What's everyone else doing? *Let's do the opposite*. Brands are associating water with life? Let's tie it to death."

Is doing the opposite the solution to every challenge? Of course not. But it's the mindset that matters—getting out of the thinking pattern that got you into a rut in the first place. I have a feeling that George Costanza would've loved to pop a can of Liquid Death during his "opposite" phase.

When Is Too Much Data...Too Much Data?

Many disciples of best practices claim that all of their decisions are "data-informed." If there's solid evidence to back up the best practice, who are we to challenge them? But to me, the best marketers are the ones who use data to *discover and test new strategies* rather than confirming existing ones.

Microsoft's brand marketing lead Jason Miller echoes this sentiment:

"When you only operate within a standard approach, you restrict the scope of meaningful testing that you can carry out—and you restrict the capacity of data to challenge received wisdom and move things forward. Truly data-driven marketers aim to establish best practice rather than just follow it—discovering for themselves what works best for their particular business and their particular audience. They are scientists trying to expand marketing's understanding rather than be limited by it."

If we all blindly obeyed existing data without testing alternatives, we'd still be producing deeply rewarding radio ads about adult diapers and riding horses named Mervin to work. But I digress.

The downside of drinking from a fire hose of data is that it becomes a crutch, a substitute for critical thinking. In recent years, the rise of data has overwhelmed brands and agencies alike, watering down advertising creative industry-wide and driving a reliance on numbers and algorithms over creativity and independent thinking.

Remember when Super Bowl advertising kicked ass? It's been a while—to the point where we now say things like, "I remember back in the day when Super Bowl ads made you laugh hard enough that you'd fart, cough, laugh, cry, write a letter to the FCC and cuddle with kittens concurrently." But with a few exceptions, Super Bowl ads have largely become yawners while ad dollars shift to more "data-informed" marketing best practices.

To me, this is synonymous with accepting defeat. Marketing has morphed into a pay-to-play proposition, leveraging technology and giving moronic influencers buckets of dollars because of a few persuasive statistics rather than fearlessly developing creative that is memorable enough to gain traction on its own. Rather than punching audiences in the face, marketers are doing things like geotargeting them or whatever the data-driven innovation of the month may be.

Now—this is important so pay close attention, bub: Does being disruptive necessitate ignoring data entirely and creating videos of waterboarding or animated characters cutting off people's heads? No, not at all. Edgy creative works for some brands that choose that path and your brand should never, ever try to be something it is not. What you can do, however, is disrupt the norm by being brave and developing a creative approach that stands out from the rest of your industry (hello, banking industry!) while remaining true to your brand's values and culture. You don't need data to tell you this; it just takes creative effort.

It's Time to Upgrade from Hand-Me-Downs

If you're not the first-born or the only child in your family, you can almost certainly relate to wearing hand-me-down clothes. Instead of starting each new kid's wardrobe from scratch, mom and dad make use of the older siblings' clothes to save time, money, and space. As the first-born in my family, my outfits eventually became my siblings' outfits. And now, as a father of four I see the same happen with my own kids. Hand-me-downs are a great starting point for any kid, but as we all know, they also have limitations.

For one thing, hand-me-downs aren't as sturdy as brand new clothes—they have wear and tear. Secondly, there's a good chance that hand-me-downs are a few years behind the latest styles or trends. Whether it's a pair of shoes or a stroller, our used stuff probably gets the job done, but there's probably something better out there. You see where I'm going with this. And let's not even get into the arguments that ensue from the child sick of the hand-me-downs. Now that I think of it, brands should throw the same fits when their agencies or in-house marketing teams try to sell a set of marketing hand-me-downs to them. It's the same thing.

When we see the shelves of a bookstore stacked with marketing playbooks or the speaker lineup at a marketing conference, most of what we're being spoon-fed is *hand-me-down content.* It goes something like this: *Hey, I did XYZ and it worked, but instead of telling you to think for yourself, I'll just repackage my old stuff and donate (or sell) it to you!*

Is this hand-me-down advice wrong? Not necessarily. There might even be a few gems in there. But don't you think you should scrutinize that secondhand advice before you copy and paste it into your own strategy? Isn't it ironic that many adults cringe at the idea of wearing someone else's clothes and obsess over the details of a used car, but when it comes to business—their *livelihood*—they're happy to gulp down secondhand advice without thinking twice?

As a rule of thumb, best practices and hand-me-downs aren't definitive ends—they're reference points. Both have their time and place, but nobody wants to live their whole life wearing their older brother's or sister's shoes.

Now, for all the recycling supporters ready to boycott this book at this point, think about this: upcycling. Take the old stuff and work with it. Remake it for today and *make it better.* Don't just cut and paste that Augmented Reality thing you read about. Think about your brand, and think about how you can repurpose the technology in a way that hasn't been considered.

–|–

When it comes to developing a brand or a marketing strategy, finding best practices should never be the goal—finding the best approach for *you* should be. If there's one thing to learn from best practices, it's that we can't place too much stock in them. Otherwise, we'd all be wearing parachute pants, eating crunchy cookies, and washing them down with hipster water in clear bottles.

So What?

1. Best practices don't make you the best. They drag you into the middle.

2. The real best practice might be the opposite of the industry standard (think soft cookies and Liquid Death.)

3. Instead of relying on data to confirm a best practice, use data to test new practices.

CHAPTER 4

Shiny Objects Don't Always Fit

There is a dangerous epidemic running rampant throughout the marketing, advertising and public relations industries. It can sabotage successful campaigns, ruin team chemistry, burn piles of cash. Nobody is safe. This epidemic is plaguing all walks of life—from interns to C-suite executives alike—and there is no cure. If this sounds horrific, that's because it is.

It's "shiny object syndrome."

Shiny object syndrome (SOS) is the tendency to chase fashionable or trendy ideas in our peripheral vision without vetting their validity. Just like you can distract a toddler with a fancy new toy, marketers are equally susceptible to being mesmerized by metaphorical toys glistening in the distance: The playbook for gaming Facebook's umpteenth algorithm, podcasts, ad tech, the hottest influencer… the list goes on. Are any of these inherently **bad**? Of course not. But blindly chasing tactic after tactic or change after change without taking the time to consider if they'll actually work is about as productive as trying to push waves back into the ocean.

Obviously SOS isn't **real** in the sense that it's a diagnosable condition. It isn't going to cause you any pain and suffering (except perhaps to your budget). But it is real in the sense that it can derail a marketing plan and waste valuable dollars. SOS is a byproduct of the urge to stay ahead of the curve and constantly improve (both good ideas). But left unchecked, SOS creates a culture of distraction in which marketers chase whatever the next "big thing" is instead of taking a step back and considering what the right thing is.

So, what's a marketer to do when their email inbox and social media feeds are overflowing with shiny objects? Should you succumb to temptation and play with all of them? Or take a step back? How are you supposed to know if those shiny objects actually fit your unique business challenge? True confession: We both have been tempted with our fair share of shiny objects. We may not have definitive answers to those questions, but we do have some stories that might make those shiny objects seem, well, not so shiny after all.

Shiny Objects: Play With Them at Your Own Risk

Let's say you're looking to hire a new employee. Your friend refers you to some hot-shot wunderkind who you're eager to invite in for an interview. He shows up looking sharp and talks a great game. He checks all the boxes: He's an impressive conversationalist, has a can-do attitude, he read that you love Mr. T and can recite his hit song "Treat Your Mother Right." He arrives bearing a pristine resume printed on leather, embroidered with Chuck Norris' fist. You've found your golden boy! But after conducting due diligence, you quickly learn that the carpet doesn't match the curtains. He didn't "choose to leave" his previous employer because his creativity was stifled. He was *asked* to leave because he was a total asshole who, in fact, hates Mr. T. This so-called top-notch writer managed nothing short of a trainwreck when he tried to string a few sentences together on a writing test. You were fortunate to find all of this out *before* you started invested in hiring and training him. That clearly saved you a lot of headaches, but there's one festering problem. Now you've got to go back to the drawing board with nothing to show but wasted time (which pisses me off more than just about anything outside of vegan cuisine).

So it goes for SOS, which is equally frustrating and futile on a variety of levels. In my own experience, I've encountered executives who are extremely adept at managing their businesses, but as gullible as Jim Jones Kool-Aid-drinkers when it comes to brand-building strategies. Maybe the executive reads something in an industry publication about a new trend in marketing. Next thing you know, you've got a CEO barging into a conference room demanding his team use doggie Snapchat filters for his B2B steel piping company. Good times. The tail is wagging the dog, and that doesn't come without consequences. The company will be left with a steaming pile of shit because some 60-year-old white dude wanted his ego assuaged after his social media-savvy granddaughter told him she loves Snapchat and stupid dog filters.

Joking aside yet militantly adhering to pro-Mr. T and Chuck Norris sentiments, I empathize with people who fall into the SOS cycle. No one is immune to it. I've fallen prey to this insidious culprit at least 4.7 times. Understandably, people think to themselves, "Here's an opportunity to be an early adopter and differentiate myself from the competition! Let's disrupt the industry!" Unfortunately, this tends to happen without properly vetting those opportunities. Rather than testing or seeking out negative feedback, they carelessly turn their valuable marketing budget into a guinea pig on steroids that looks like Mark Wahlberg and smells like seaweed.

Shiny objects are shiny for a reason. They're new, alluring and often reinforced by the media, consultants, and influencers. But every shiny object should come with a warning label that says, "Play at Your Own Risk Because There's a Good Chance You'll Flush a Lot of Dough Down the Toilet" followed by this list of potential risks:

- **Wasting money:** The market is flooded with tools, services and software that are impressive and undoubtedly fun to use. But each of these new additions comes with a price tag, and hopping from one to another can rack up an impressive credit card bill while you're left with some unimpressive results.

- **Wasting time:** Have you ever gone to Target to buy a light bulb, then found yourself on the opposite end of the store an hour later wondering if you need a bean bag chair and a lava lamp for your living room? That's SOS in action. It's never been easier to go down the rabbit hole of potentially cool ideas while the clock keeps on ticking in the background.

- **Confusing your team:** If you're obsessed with podcasting on Monday, suggest a viral video campaign on Wednesday and shift your budget to YouTube pre-roll on Friday, your team can never keep up. When the goal post keeps moving, people never know where to aim, causing frustration, confusion, and diminished productivity.

- **Project graveyards:** We all know a guy who has a garage littered with incomplete projects, like your neighbor who tried building a sailboat but two years later has a less-than-seaworthy pile of lumber in his garage. As soon as he makes headway on a task, a new problem catches his eye. Meanwhile, he never completes anything. In that same vein, marketers often fixate on a fad—until something better comes along. Rather than mining one solid strategy to its fullest potential, they flit from one shallow mine to another.

Of course, no guru has the gall to slap a warning label on their Ted Talk, online course or book. That means it's up to you (and me) to put them to the test.

Shiny Objects Themselves Aren't to Blame

Hamburgers on their own don't cause obesity. Eating a hamburger at lunch every day for can pack on the pounds. Liquor on its own can't cause liver disease. Drinking heavily for decades can. A smartphone in your pocket doesn't cause tech addiction. Staring at it for eight hours a day might. All of this is to say, exciting or fun things can bring pleasure into your life, until they don't. They aren't inherently bad—it's *how we use them* that determines our fate.

I was reminded of this lesson while listening to a podcast where the host was discussing the relationship between startup founders and consultants. Early-stage founders usually round up five advisors who have run successful businesses and pick their brains for actionable advice. More often than not, the eager entrepreneurs are on the lookout for a silver bullet that can boost their business overnight. But this creates a sticky situation.

Let's say you land the founder of Domino's on your advisory board. Great news, right? Now, this fine gentleman might have some evergreen insights about building a brand or acquiring customers, but when it comes to developing a detailed strategy, they will be speaking two different languages. Domino's was founded in 1960 before social media, apps, and review sites existed. As a matter of fact, the internet *itself* wasn't even a thing back then. He was building his brand with a completely different set of tools. You actually were forced to pick up a phone and order a pizza by *talking to a human being.* Accordingly, his tricks and tips run the risk of being taken out of context and unaligned with the founder's new, unique business goal.

Now, let's take a step back here. Does this mean the advice coming from the founder of Domino's is "wrong?" Not necessarily. Just as hamburgers, vodka, and smartphones don't cause diseases on their own, shiny marketing objects don't cause catastrophic business failures on their own. It's *how we use them* that matters. It's the context in which the advice or the tactic is being used. The marketing influencers, viral videos, events, street teams and social justice campaigns are neutral. They can't produce problems (or solutions) unless you include them in your one-of-a-kind equations.

Look, I know we've been debunking formulas and giving gurus a hard time throughout this book. But I want to make an important distinction here: There are plenty of well-intentioned marketing consultants and authors out there. Most of them aren't hawking snake oil just to make a quick buck. More than likely, they're simply looking to capitalize on the success they've had. And who can fault them for that?

But here's the caveat: It's your responsibility (yes, yours) to scrutinize what they have to say. Just because it's cool, shiny, or new doesn't mean it's good for you. To give another food analogy, check the ingredient label and the nutrition facts and decide if it fits your diet. Blaming Facebook for your brand's failed marketing campaign is about as dumb as suing Skippy if you have a peanut allergy or taking McDonald's to court because it caused you to gain 50 pounds. In case you forgot, the "McLawsuit" was a real thing in 2003, and it failed.

How you market your product is different than how someone in another industry with a different product markets theirs. Whatever worked for them may not necessarily work for you. In fact, it probably won't—unless you're both pushing reversible Nic Cage sequin pillows through Buzzfeed lists. Now that's foolproof.

Sexy Results Don't Always Require Sexy Tactics

Let's be honest: Marketing, advertising and public relations industries have sex appeal. TV dramas like **Mad Men** are able to make a storyboard concept session exciting. There are entire publications devoted to covering the latest eye-grabbing, thumb-stopping campaigns. The simple fact that these industries are worth upwards of a trillion dollars is, in itself, worth gawking over. But for all the hype surrounding the latest ad tech and glitzy videos, it's the not-so-sexy tactics that often yield sexy results.

Let me explain with an analogy. But first, some context.

You're not going to see a blockbuster summer movie about search engine optimization (SEO) anytime soon. However, it is one of the most data-centric means of marketing available today. It allows us to analyze cause and effect within the primary platform on which most human beings today find their information: Search engines. Think about how many times a week you do a Google search. While SEO can be a useful ingredient in brand's custom marketing cocktail, it's far from sexy. In fact, it's the antithesis of a shiny object.

SEO is like the guy with a wooden leg, massive facial scar and roving left eye at a dinner party. You see him standing alone, not looking so great. On the other side of the room is the life of the party: The stunning, glamorous guy or gal that everyone is trying to talk to and take selfies with. You don't have the patience to mingle with the crowd, so you decide to strike up a conversation with the loner although you don't know what to look at with the whole roving eye thing. Lo and behold, it ends up being the best decision you made. As soon as you strike up a conversation, you realize how pleasant and fascinating he is. Before you know it, you're ten fishing trips deep. Meanwhile, nobody got anywhere with the fan favorite everyone flocked to who really sucked and had terrible breath anyway. Symmetrical eyes notwithstanding, it turns out that person was vapid and didn't know the difference between a walrus and horseshoe mustache.

Obviously, SEO isn't the only un-sexy tactic that can outperform whatever the flavor of the month is. The reason I make that analogy is because it perfectly illustrates a dilemma we faced a few years ago that ended in a failed pitch and ultimately a failed business.

We were called by a popular, very large podcast platform that was founded as a division of **Slate Magazine** and eventually spun off into its own unique property. It had a number of popular original podcasts, including Malcolm Gladwell's Revisionist History. In my initial conversation with their marketing director, I asked if he had ever considered investing in search, to which he replied, "No." I immediately pooped my shorts.

I used the dinner party analogy and made my case. "When people are looking for podcasts, they're not Googling your platform's name," I said. "They're Googling 'podcasts about karate or prison or food or pooping." I told him I couldn't think of a better solution for his specific problem, regardless of whether or not that solution made his company or us look "cool."

That conversation earned us an invitation to New York to pitch our strategy—and our approach was a mix of SEO, content creation, paid social and earned media. Unsexy, perhaps, but logical, measurable tactics. Well, we lost that pitch to the agency we were competing against because, as their marketing director told me, they wanted a "traditional media relations agency." The company felt that showing up in the headlines for a few hours mattered more than showing up when it mattered most: when prospective listeners were looking for new podcasts. Less than a year later, that platform ceased to produce original content and was in the toilet.

Shiny objects aren't just distracting, they're destructive.

Solutions Looking for Problems

Two years ago, a couple guys pitched me a startup idea and told me to think of it as Grubhub for the golf course. Grubhub, of course, is the popular mobile food ordering app that connects users to local takeout restaurants. These guys wanted to apply the same concept for golfers. Let's say you're on hole four and you're craving a cocktail or a plate of hot wings. Rather than waiting until turn nine, this app would let you order anything from your clubhouse and have it delivered via golf cart by the time it takes to play two holes.

Sounds sweet, right?

But as they discussed their big idea with golfers, their hopes were quickly dampened. "That's cool, but I don't need that," said one. "I usually wait until the ninth hole, otherwise I'll pack a granola bar or bring a flask. What am I supposed to do, sit and eat a plate of hot wings on the tee box while people back up behind me?"

More and more golfers echoed this sentiment. It quickly dawned on them that their idea which seemed like magic on paper didn't address a real need for their user base. In fact, it might have created more problems than solutions. As you can imagine, nobody invested in "Grubhub for the green" and the idea fell through.

Just like that startup idea was a solution looking for a problem, shiny objects in marketing often try to solve problems that don't exist. Take podcasting, one of the hottest marketing trends of the 21st century. As I write this, there are more people making podcasts than listening to them. And yet, thousands of people continue to launch them because it seems smart, cool, or hip. Never mind if their audience (if they have one) *wants* a podcast or if the host even has anything to say that's worth a damn.

In 2016, Jordan Harbinger, host of The Art of Charm (a top 50 podcast on iTunes), made a controversial statement at a conference packed with entrepreneurs, authors, and public figures. He told them that they should *not* start a podcast. Why? Because the world would be a better place if less people conducted amateur interviews to make a soft sell for their brands.

"When everyone is talking about some trend, the smart money ignores it and does the opposite," says Ryan Holiday, author of *Perennial Seller: The Art of Making and Marketing Work that Lasts*. "Meanwhile, it's the lazy, the selfish and the lame that try to imitate and cash in."

I don't have a podcast about marketing, although I'm sure launching one would be fun. But if thousands of entrepreneurs are fixating on the podcast gold rush, I'd rather channel my energy elsewhere. More importantly, what good is it to solve a problem that doesn't exist? The way I see it, podcasting wouldn't help me get anything besides a quick ego boost and a cool, broadcast-grade microphone.

Don't get me wrong, there's a time and place for a little razzle-dazzle. But if you bank your entire strategy on sizzle without steak, everybody goes hungry.

Take It From Jeff Bezos

As I type this passage, Instagram is rolling out QR codes that open up AR filters and adding Stories to its Explore tab. Facebook is tweaking its sponsored messages feature and altering its algorithm to promote "worthwhile and close friend content." Snapchat just released baby and gender swap filters. Twitter is adding GIF, poll and emoji support to TweetDeck and rewriting its user guidelines for the billionth time.

For marketers, it's easy to become obsessed (or terrified) by the ceaseless flood of social media updates that saturate tech blogs on a daily basis. It seems impossible to stay up-to-date with every new trend, update, or modification—much less mastering them or successfully incorporating them into an integrated marketing communications plan. I'm not suggesting we should all become Luddites and revert to faxing press releases and using sandwich boards (although a good sandwich board is as appealing as a good sandwich). There's certainly something to be said for the ability to adapt to changes within the industry. After all, that's why we founded Elasticity in the first place. It's cool to be the first brand to do "X" and to be seen as an innovating, disruptive force. It's liberating to believe that you're putting the client in the best position to succeed. But when you give more weight to trend-chasing and instant gratification than foresight and long-term value, your sense of autonomy is quickly lost.

The author Robert Greene calls this being in "tactical hell." By that, he means you're stuck in a state of being perpetually reactive to the demands and whims of other people or organizations (like owning an agency!). You're driven by emotional impulses instead of logical or strategic ones, fighting battle after trivial battle. This is where a critical lesson from Amazon CEO Jeff Bezos comes into play. He has repeated this mantra in a number of industry addresses:

Focus on the things that don't change.

"I very frequently get the question: 'What's going to change in the next 10 years?'" Bezos said. "And that is a very interesting question; it's a very common one. I almost never get the question: 'What's not going to change in the next 10 years?' And I submit to you that that second question is actually the more important of the two, because you can build a business strategy around the things that are stable in time."

This simple premise is incredibly easy to forget when novelty seems to be the secret to success. Catching the next wave, predicting the next trend, hacking algorithms—these make for great headlines, but not great strategies. Many people, including marketers, are not strategic. Instead they are reactive, chasing one fad after another without a plan, a vision or sense of how one decision impacts the next. They may be working hard, experimenting with every new update and tweaking their blog posts to squeeze every drop of SEO juice they can out of them. But more often than not, shortcuts yield short-term benefits. We forget that technology can't compensate for big ideas and sound strategies. It can only supplement them.

Bezos addressed the seductiveness of short-sighted thinking in a letter to his shareholders nearly two decades ago: "We believe that a fundamental measure of our success will be the shareholder value we create over the long term." He went on to explain that Amazon would always focus on the longer term, "rather than short-term profitability or short-term Wall Street reactions."

Bezos understands that real value lies in thinking decades ahead, not giving in to the shiny keys jingling in our peripheral vision. He understands that business isn't about what's new. Rather, it's about **what works**. His maxim, to focus on the things that don't change, is perennially true. It's held up through years past, and will not change in the years to come.

Start Tinkering

In 2005, a self-taught software engineer named Gever Tulley decided he was fed up with the prototypical education system. His main beef was its emphasis on linear thinking, which he felt caused curiosity and creativity to wither. To combat this, Tulley created a summer program that flipped education upside down. He called it Tinkering School.

Tinkering School is a week-long program near San Francisco where kids learn through experimentation and action rather than lectures and instructions. Participants deconstruct appliances, break stuff, and build contraptions including roller coasters and three-story tree houses. There is no curriculum. There are no tests or evaluations. There aren't even set subjects. Tinkering School is "learning by doing" incarnated. If your kid likes to take things apart (like your $1,500 MacBook Pro), don't scold him or her. Your kid might have the right stuff to be the next Wozniak. Instead, putting your child on a plane to San Francisco might be the smartest move you can make to realize their potential.

Tinker School is a perfect analogy for how we can approach shiny objects. For many marketers, there are two ways to approach the latest and greatest industry innovations: turn a blind eye to them because they're probably too good to be true, or fall head over heels and blindly embrace them. But this binary thinking is dangerous. It either seals you off from new ideas or constantly distracts you with the new flavor of the month. Rather, we should take notes from the tinkerers: Instead of taking the shiny object at face value, "take it apart" just like a curious kid takes apart a video game console. By breaking it down into its individual components, you see how it works. Accordingly, you have control over it instead of letting it control you.

Let's take influencer marketing for example. Right this minute, influencers are some of the shiniest objects in the world of marketing, but they come with jaw-dropping price tags. Some influencers charge upwards of six figures for a single Instagram post, and there's enough data to persuade you that this is an easy (but expensive) means to get eyeballs on your product. This signals that influencers must "work."

There's a whole other book that will be written as the days of the instagram influencer are numbered. When an "influencer" with 2.5 million followers can't sell 15 tee-shirts, you need to take notice. When moms are getting their husbands to quit their jobs and follow them around with a camera all day, only to get free product for themselves with no discernable ROI? Well, that's not a sustainable marketing tactic that will last much longer.

Let's get back to tinkerers. Because a tinkerer doesn't think like that.

A tinkerer breaks down influencer marketing into its individual parts to see how they fit together, and how that applies to their client or brand. Is it "influencer marketing" as a whole that drives results, or is it just third party validation in general? Or is it portraying the product in a new context? Or is it reaching a new audience? All of these are pieces of the influencer marketing puzzle, but you might only need one piece for your particular problem—and the only way to find that out is by tinkering.

So, before you throw that shiny object in the trash or show it off to your team, take it apart. Examine it closely. Work backwards. It may seem silly, but it can save you plenty of time, money, and heartache.

Grab a Chainsaw

"If you want to carve an elephant from a block of wood, you don't start the process with fine-grit sandpaper."

Carl Richards made use of this metaphor in his "Sketch Guy" column in **The New York Times**. Richards is a personal finance wiz, but the metaphor has equally strong implications when it comes to marketing. A brand is a sculpture, and if you want to carve a masterpiece you'll need to start with blunt instruments and broad strokes. Unfortunately, we don't have to look far to see the marketing equivalent of carving with sandpaper:

- Obsessing over the minutiae of color palettes and fonts when people have no idea what the brand stands for.
- Starting a #Hashtag! when the brand has no followers.
- "Optimizing" content for SEO when that content sucks to begin with.
- Sending "news" releases when the brand hasn't done anything worth talking about.
- Buying a Snapchat filter for an event that nobody knows about.

When brands fall victim to SOS, they're tempted to tinker with the sexy facets of marketing while the difficult and important questions are left unattended. And who can blame them? Read the headlines in the top marketing and branding publications and count how many sensationalized, hyper-specific, sandpaper strategies you can find. Ironically, though, popular isn't usually productive.

"You know what trying to sand an elephant out of a block of wood actually is? It's daunting," says Richards. "And what daunting means is that you're probably going to quit before you even start. Maybe you'll take a few passes, and perhaps you'll get as far as shaping a leg or a trunk. But eventually you're going to give up. The process is just too slow."

I couldn't have said it better myself.

The funny thing about the alternative—the chainsaw approach—is that once you start hacking away, you realize your brand can evolve into something much different (and better) than what was originally intended. Take Instagram for example. It started out as Burbn: an app that let users check in to particular locations, make plans for future check-ins, earn points for hanging out with friends and post pictures of their meet-ups. This was too complicated, though. Burbn had too many features. But the developers noticed something interesting. The one feature people actually used on the app was photo-sharing.

So, what did Burbn do? Share a bunch of platitudes on social media about friendship? Change the interface of the app to make it more appealing? Chase influencers and reporters? Wrong, wrong and wrong. They zeroed in on the photo-sharing feature and scrapped everything else. The result is the billion-user Instagram we know today.

It's only after making those initial violent chops that sandpaper can be effective. Now, grab your proverbial chainsaw and go wild.

–|–

By the time you pick up this book, the marketing flavor of the month will be drastically different than what it was when we were writing it. But that's the point. If you browse the Amazon archives, you'll see all sorts of once-shiny artifacts, from guides to display advertising to press release playbooks. These might have once been beneficial, but new technology and new audiences inevitably made them irrelevant. Shiny objects are timely. But cultivating the mindset to vet them for legitimacy is time*less*.

So What?

1. Just because an object is shiny doesn't mean it's the right shape.

2. Shiny objects can't compensate for big ideas and sound strategies, they can only supplement them.

3. Shiny objects aren't inherently dangerous—it's the context in which they're used that determines results.

4. Break down the shiny object to figure out which (if any) of its components are valid.

CHAPTER 5

Risky Business

In the decades following World War II, American consumers wanted to show the world that they were the world's superpower. This collective mindset crossed over into the automotive industry, sparking the popularity of muscle cars such as the Chevrolet Corvette.

How, then, was a company with a name like Volkswagen supposed to sell its strange-looking Beetle which was designed and built in Nazi Germany?

Advertising agencies in the 1960s were accustomed to creating information-heavy content with fantastical visuals to sell cars. But DDB (Volkswagen's agency) knew that wouldn't cut it. They had to come up with an idea that would stand out from the pack. DDB took a gamble not only with its creative direction, but with its entire approach to how advertising was produced. While most agencies had copywriters and artists on separate floors, William Bernbach (DDB's cofounder) placed his agency's copywriters and artists side by side—sparking what's now called "the creative revolution." But this new agency model wasn't just smoke and mirrors: It gave birth to the ad that changed advertising forever. The tagline, which doubled as a call to action was simply "Think Small."

The "Think Small" campaign broke the mold of advertising as the world knew it in a few ways. It used a sans-serif font when everyone else was using serif fonts. It referenced widows and orphans instead of stunning celebrities. It reverted to black and white when color was chic. And perhaps strangest of all, the ad consisted almost entirely of unused white space. When most people take risks, they might consider a small tweak here or there. But DDB rebooted the entire system.

"[The ad] did much more than boost sales and build a lifetime of brand loyalty," noted *The Portland Business Journal.* "The ad, and the work of the ad agency behind it, *changed the very nature of advertising*—from the way it's created to what you see as a consumer today." (emphasis ours)

There are entire books written about those two words—"Think Small"—which don't even make grammatical sense when put together. And if we're being honest, Apple's famous "Think Different" slogan was simply a resurrected version of Volkswagen's "Think Small." Nike went in a similar direction with its memorable "Just Do It." For Volkswagen, DDB's campaign proved the power of zigging when everyone else zagged—even at the risk of a big idea turning into a big nothing-burger. And make no mistake, this was a risky move. A major retooling of an ad strategy for a national brand carries with it tens of millions of dollars. One need only read Randall Rothenberg's *Where the Suckers Moon,* which traces the missteps of the hip ad agency Wieden+Kennedy in its ill-conceived advertising strategy to make Subaru a household name in 1991. It was during the recession, and the agency's creative director despised cars. A multi-car pileup ensued.

Throughout the previous four chapters, we've discussed the problems with best practices, the value of lateral thinking, and our beef with gurus. With all of that considered, we'd be naive not to address the elephant in the room: risk. Blazing a new trail like DDB's sounds great in theory, but when the rubber meets the road, stepping out of your comfort zone can be terrifying. Not to mention, it raises a lot of questions:

- Is it worth it for a brand to do a 180 and risk its 100-year-old reputation?
- What are the varying degrees of risk?
- Is it ok to piss people off?
- Is any publicity good publicity?

These are the questions we'll explore.

Teaching Old Dogs New Tricks

Prior to 2010, Old Spice was synonymous with old age. Founded in 1934, and inspired by a woman's potpourri, the grooming products were a mainstay for any guy with gray hair grasping for one last shot at youth. But Old Spice's brand managers began to panic in the early 2000s. On top of being associated with old, stale, pale males, Old Spice was getting its lunch eaten by Axe, the bro-branded body wash that was quickly becoming the bathing product of choice for young men. If Old Spice was to transform its stodgy persona, it needed to take a risk.

That's where Wieden+Kennedy came in.

Rather than force-feeding Old Spice's old brand down the throats of indifferent millennials, the Portland-based ad agency tore the old playbook to shreds and embarked on a seemingly insane idea: get an attractive dude named Isaiah Mustafa to rattle off witty dialogue and film him in a bathroom that turned into a boat, that turned into a horse.

Imagine convincing a brand manager from the 1940s to jump on board with that—but that's the point. New generations respond to new messages, and disseminating those messages often entails risk, especially if the brand already has a negative or neutral perception.

"[The campaign] took an old, sleepy brand and woke it up," said Mark Tutssel, jury president of the Cannes Lions International Advertising Festival.

Old Spice isn't the only proverbial old dog that's been taught new tricks over the past several years. Take H&R Block. You know, big green box, old white dudes from Kansas City wearing ties, wearing eye-shades and tip-tapping on calculators. Leading up to tax season in 2014, our team at Elasticity was tasked with building brand engagement with 21-to 35-year-olds—an audience that increasingly saw the brand as stodgy and stale in light of Turbo Tax and other competitors. Our work was certainly cut out for us, so what could we possibly do? Pour millions of dollars into TV spots? Meh. Inundate Facebook with paid ads? Been there, done that. Pitch a bunch of reporters about why H&R Block is "progressive?" Yawn.

What about manufacturing a fictitious crisis amongst annoying hipsters? A *Hipster Tax Crisis*, if you will.

Based on insights from our previous Stache Act campaign for H&R Block (where we manufactured a piece of faux legislature demanding a tax break for mustached Americans), we knew that any effort needed to be highly disruptive, even at the risk of pissing a few people off, in order to reach the right audience at the right time on the right platforms. To that end, we dove into the deep end in order to leverage the widespread backlash against the hipster subculture in America—creating a fictitious "Hipster Tax Crisis."

The premise was simple:

It's a dirty little secret that no one wants to talk about, but the American Hipster is in a deep crisis—a Hipster Tax Crisis. That's right, they are struggling to properly file taxes in non-ironic fashion. Blankets do not qualify as deductible clothing expenses, scarves cannot be counted as dependents, kale grown on a fire escape doesn't qualify for farm tax credits (total bummer, by the way).

To increase the engagement, we enlisted sardonic ESPN SportsCenter anchor Kenny Mayne to serve as the face of the campaign, as well as the Upright Citizens Brigade comedy troupe. Then we aligned the campaign with Covenant House, a national nonprofit dedicated to helping homeless youth. At the center of the campaign, we created a humorous microsite, spread videos of Kenny Mayne and Upright Citizens Brigade players to deepen brand affinity. The microsite hit numerous touch points to drive engagement including Hipster Tax Facts and a HipsterizeMe photo application.

The campaign culminated in the 'Irony Games' in Seattle: a celebration of the American hipster where the greatest hipster in history was announced. You know you're on the right track when a campaign gets life through news reporting. We achieved that. The campaign was supported by extensive earned media rather than paid advertisements because H&R Block was busy wasting their real money having an old white guy in a bowtie pitch his personality to other old white people who already liked Block.

The campaign generated thousands of engagement points and hundreds of earned media placements either loving or hating the campaign. In fact, half of the story that ensued (beyond the wildly popular movement) was that a sleepy "your dad's tax shop" would even *try* something so wacky in the first place. The subsequent press and the popularity of the movement culminated in a competitor announcing on a Wall Street earnings call that they missed their mark due to an unforeseen aggressive digital campaign directed at a core target audience of theirs.

Now, had we played it safe, we'd only have accelerated a downward spiral for the brand.

Some gaps in business require a leap of faith. In order to cross the delta, you have to set aside your preconceived notions and be willing to roll with the punches. It's incumbent upon marketers to bring risky ideas to the table. If we don't, we're nothing more than cowards. Was there any guarantee that Isaiah Mustafa could sell soap for Old Spice or that making fun of hipsters could sell tax services? Nope. But you can bet your ass Wieden+Kennedy and Elasticity were willing to go down swinging.

Gambling With Coffee Beans

In 2012, a man by the name of Mike Brown in Saratoga Springs, New York took the biggest risk of his life. After getting fed up with the multitude of chic, hipster-esque coffee brands smattered across America, he decided to throw a wrench in the system. Instead of branding his coffee with soothing colors, he opted for black. Instead of giving his coffee an "artisanal" feel, he slapped a minimal skull and crossbones icon on his packaging. Instead of posting pictures of cardigan-clad millennials sipping lattes, he launched a podcast called Fueled by Death with guests including the raunchy/contro-versial comedian Bill Burr. And, most importantly, he doubled his competitor's caffeine content.

He called it Death Wish Coffee.

Based on a hunch, Mike Brown created the anti-coffee brand. Who would've guessed that death-branded coffee could come to life? Coffee already gives people the jitters. Why double the dosage? But Death Wish was an instant hit. It won Intuit's "Small Business, Big Game competition, which earned the brand a free commercial during Super Bowl 50. Death Wish was even freeze dried and sent to the International Space Station to keep astronauts alert. In hindsight, Brown's risk was a brilliant one—like saying "hit me" when you have 19 in blackjack and getting dealt a 2. Except it wasn't a risk at all.

What I just described isn't the true story behind Death Wish Coffee. This is.

Prior to 2012, Mike Brown was hearing from a lot of truckers and other blue collar workers who were always tired, but never wanted to stop working. These are the people we refer to as "the backbone of America," and as Brown quickly discovered, they weren't drinking Starbucks to get their caffeine fix. In fact, they bemoaned the entire "coffee shop" aesthetic. They didn't care about wi-fi and sous vide egg white bites. Instead of grabbing a coffee in the morning (or at midnight), they grabbed a Red Bull or a Monster. But that was growing old. All these people wanted was a ton of caffeine from a brand that spoke their language. That's how Death Wish Coffee was born.

To outsiders, launching Death Wish Coffee appeared risky and unfounded. There seemed to be no precedent for it. Truthfully, though, it was a voice for an audience that felt like it wasn't being spoken to. Mike Brown didn't look at Starbucks and say, "Let's be rebels"—what he did was look at an audience and gave them what they wanted. If people outside that circle thought it was weird or risky, so be it.

"When you pay more attention to the customer than to the industry, the customer pays more attention to you," says Jay Acunzo, who documents Death Wish's brand story in his book **Break the Wheel**. "It seems crazy from the outside looking in until you hear the context. Then, it sounds smart, strategic, and logical."

If a marketing decision feels radical, you might be paying too much attention to the competition. Rather than solely marketing yourself as the anti-brand (which is unquestionably risky), you should be **for** something (think Death Wish being for the untapped blue collar market). With this insight in mind, most of the successful "risky" campaigns we see in the headlines aren't so risky after all.

Authentically Inauthentic

Let's take a moment to talk about the "world's worst hostel." The world's worst hostel has two locations in Portugal and Amsterdam. The brand's official title is Hans Brinker Hostel, but in today's cluttered media environment, that name just doesn't cut it. Instead, Hans Brinker carved out an unofficial tagline: "the world's worst hostel," pandering to cash-strapped travellers who tend to care more about inebriating themselves rather than receiving a complimentary bathrobe or a mint on their pillow. Hans Brinker even embraced it's reputation to the extent that it published an ad with cigarette butts smeared into a patch of shabby carpet: "Hans Brinker Budget Hotel. It Can't Get Any Worse. But We'll Do Our Best.

Seems risky, right? Except there's one slight problem: Hans Brinker's advertising is nothing more than a gimmick.

If you stay at a Hans Brinker Hostel, you'll notice that it's actually not that bad—and it's definitely not the worst in the world. They offer free breakfast, package deals, a bar, and nightclub which stays open every day of the week, all for about $100 a night. The managers even *apologize* for poor experiences on review sites such as Yelp and TripAdvisor. If you're the "world's worst hostel," why wouldn't you say something like, "What'd you expect? We're the worst hostel in the world."?

When it comes to risky marketing, Hans Brinker talks the talk, but doesn't walk the walk.

Now, let's talk about the world's worst restaurant chain: Dick's Last Resort. Since 1985, Dick's has been "putting the F.U. in fun" at several locations throughout the country. How? They embarrass their patrons by adorning them in giant hats that say things such as "underwear model for Depends" and hurling sarcastic comments left and right. The restaurant relies on insulting its customers to make money—and it works. Dick's Last Resort is exactly what it promises to be: a terrible, yet somehow amazing, experience.

So, here we have two brands—Hans Brinker and Dick's Last Resort—that both likely sat around a conference room table and thought, *we need to take a risk*. One of those brands took a risk and followed through with it. The other walked to the edge of the cliff, posted a picture, then retreated to safety. You know which is which.

There's nothing worse than a person (or a brand) that says they're something that they're not. Job number one for any organization is being authentic—true to what you stand for, to what you tell your employees, and how you articulate your value proposition to customers. If you aren't, eventually your employees will become dismayed and your customers will be dissatisfied. Let's get something straight: Being authentic doesn't mean you're kind, caring, or down to earth. Being authentic means you're *true to yourself*. You can be an authentic asshole, as long as you don't deviate from the qualities that make you an asshole.

So, are you ready to take that big gamble on your next marketing campaign? Great. But please, for the love of all things holy, *own it*.

"We F!!cked Up:" a Tale of Two Apologies

Prior to 2009, Domino's Pizza sucked. Like, really bad. As one reporter remarked, "[The pizza] tasted like it had been frozen, recycled, and then left out in the sun all day." But journalists weren't the only folks who were having a field day slandering the pizza chain. Here are some more critiques from focus group participants and angry tweeters:

"Domino's pizza crust, to me, is like cardboard."

"Worst excuse for pizza I've ever had...the sauce tastes like ketchup."

"Low quality and forgettable."

"I think Domino's pizza is made by machines...human hands probably don't even touch it."

On top of this PR shit-show, Domino's' stock price had toppled to a measly eight dollars per share. It was clear that action had to be taken. Most brands in this scenario would have kept those nasty comments locked in a safe at their corporate headquarters while tasking an agency with concocting some distraction to salvage their reputation. Domino's, however, turned shit to sugar with an ad campaign for the ages: "Oh, Yes We Did."

Rather than circumventing it's scathing criticisms, Domino's leaned into them. The campaign kicked off with a newly-minted CEO appearing on camera and bluntly admitting that his pizza sucks...

well, used to suck. The ads directly quoted furious customers and plastered the insults on screens across the globe. But it didn't stop there: Domino's required employees to undergo quality training to ensure its pizza never dipped below consumers' standards again. They even hand-delivered their new-and-improved pizzas to the haters and got their stamp of approval.

Admitting your product sucks and asking everyone to try it again is a risk that would scare the hell out of most executives. Keep in mind, the brand was nearly five decades old at the time—it's not like they had nothing to lose. The Domino's exec who green-lighted the campaign probably raised the eyebrows of his fellow senior managers. But when the rebrand was said and done, Domino's had gone from being a punchline about quality to the second-largest pizza chain in the world and a stock market darling.

Now, let's switch gears and talk about another brand that made a grade-A f!!ck-up: Wells Fargo.

It all started in September 2016 when news broke that the bank opened more than a million accounts, some of which had fake names. A flood of fines ensued, rising to more than $1 billion for making auto-loan clients pay for unwanted insurance among other shady tactics.

In response to the crisis at hand, Wells Fargo admitted it lost the trust of its constituents. Then, 3,500 employees were ousted and a clean sweep of the board was made. Nothing to see here, right? On paper, this appears to be the same approach that Domino's took: Atone for your faults and replace the bad guys with good guys. But I'll venture to say you're far more fond of Domino's than Wells Fargo. Why is that? One word: execution.

Wells Fargo's crisis response campaign didn't make audiences feel better—it confused them. "Established 1852, reestablished 2018," read the ads. "Today is a new day." The campaign promised to right the brand's wrongs, but conveniently forgot to mention what was wrong in the first place. What were they apologizing for? If a person saw the ads out of context, they'd have no idea. By contrast, Domino's put their screw-up front and center, owned it and took responsibility.

PR News put it simply: Wells Fargo doesn't get it.

Just like Hans Brinker doesn't live up to the "world's worst hostel" reputation that it leans on, Wells Fargo's pseudo-candor has gone over like a lead balloon with audiences. So, what should these stuffy bankers learn from one of America's favorite pizza chain? If you want to stick your neck out, you better stick it out all the way, because everybody's watching.

The Right Risk for the Right Brand

I spent several years working with UPS, one of the most risk averse brands in the history of civilization. Its culture is almost military-esque. There's a process for how you drive your trucks, how you deliver a package, how you go to the bathroom, and so on. UPS has built a wildly successful business on its systematic nature, but there's always wiggle room. For example, I once suggested they turn their trucks into billboards since they'd have countless square feet of free advertising real estate. But that was an anathema to UPS. How dare I besmirch their beautiful, brown trucks with anything other than the letters U-P-S on a bland chocolate sea?

But I digress.

Risk is all about context. There's a fine line between using UPS trucks as billboards and having UPS drivers blow confetti in the faces of package recipients. Both are edgy; but only one aligns with the brand's value proposition. Simply pulling the fire alarm just for the sake of being disruptive is as annoying as a spoiled brat screaming for attention.

Speaking of spoiled brats, let's talk about Kendall Jenner and her trainwreck of a Pepsi ad.

You probably recall the cola crisis that ensued after a tone deaf commercial appropriated images from Black Lives Matter protests to sell soda. Pepsi quickly pulled the spot after intense criticism while the 21-year-old Jenner sobbed about the incident in the 14th season of E!'s remarkably unremarkable "Keeping Up With the Kardashians."

Pepsi is the last brand that should have stuck its neck out like that, especially in the tone deaf manner in which it did. Ben and Jerry's, on the other hand, has carved out a reputation for its progressive social commentary with tweets such as, "It's hard to celebrate 4/20 when so many people of color are still being arrested for pot. We have to do better."

When it comes to publishing risky content, there are generally two factors at play: authenticity and audience. Pepsi doesn't give a shit about social justice and was speaking to an audience of billions who may or may not have agreed with the brand's stance. Ben and Jerry's actually takes action on behalf of social justice and knows for a fact that it's audience cares too. Michael Serazio, a professor of communications at Boston College and author of *Your Ad Here* explains this nuance.

"For decades, most advertisers didn't want to get involved with risk at all," says Serazio. "They wanted to sell to Republicans and Democrats alike. They didn't want to piss anyone off. They wanted everybody to just have a Coke and a smile. Now, we're entering a really interesting period in which brands don't need the mass, they just need the niche. And if you're going to chase the niche as opposed to the mass, then you have to commit yourself to a specific political platform."

If a brand comes to us and says they want to run something risky, my first question is the same as if they want to run something conservative: Why? What's the insight behind your instinct? Is there data to back up the idea? If there are solid answers to these questions, I can get on board. But if the risk is unfounded or misaligned with the brand's character, I politely guide him or her back to the drawing board.

Strawberries, Jalapenos, and Tommy Hilfiger

A couple blocks from our office in St. Louis is a frozen yogurt shop that has a reputation for coming up with exotic flavor combinations. The owners started with a controversial strawberry-jalapeno concoction that they adapted from a dessert they tried in Texas. Not long after that, they introduced the world's first Red Hot Riplet frozen yogurt, which combined the spicy mesquite flavor of a beloved local potato chip brand with sweet vanilla yogurt. At first, people thought the guys were simply throwing arbitrary flavors together to grab attention. But after a few early adopters got a taste, people realized there was a method behind the madness.

Specific flavor profiles complement each other to create distinct tastes that are unfamiliar, but strangely delicious. For example, vanilla and strawberry yogurt both mesh well with a hint of heat. Infusing frozen yogurt with ketchup, mustard, relish, and mayo is risky (and in all likelihood disgusting). Infusing frozen yogurt with flavors that make you do a double take and think, "Hmm, maybe that will taste good," is savvy. In other words, if you're going to stir up controversy through differentiation, your product or service better have legs to stand on its own.

Speaking of controversy, do you know how Tommy Hilfiger got his foot in the door of the fashion industry?

In 1985, Tommy Hilfiger was a young designer with a boyish grin, a weird name, and a store on the Upper West Side of Manhattan that nobody knew about. Hilfiger's initial idea for an ad campaign was to take some young models to the Hamptons and photograph them against the ocean. After all, that's the standard his idols— Armani, Versace, and Calvin Klein—set. But Hilfiger's outrageous ad man, George Lois, wasn't having it.

"Are you crazy?" said Lois. "It will take you 20 years to build a brand that way." To prove his point, he asked Hilfiger to identify the ads for Armani and Versace without names or logos. It was impossible. To get people to recognize Tommy Hilfiger, George Lois devised a simple yet radical concept.

The 4 Great American Designers for Men Are:

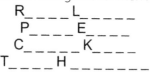

This is the logo of the least known of the four

"I told him I wouldn't do it and that it was embarrassing and obnoxious," said Hilfiger, "but my partners pointed out that we didn't have a lot of money at the time and had to get the name out there as effectively as we could so I reluctantly agreed. It was the first time I considered quitting the business and putting my head in the sand."

It's a good thing Tommy eventually let George follow through with the idea, because it put him on the lips (and backs) of millions on a mere $200,000 budget. The ad, spelled out in 10-foot-high letters overlooking New York's Times Square, sparked an avalanche of national publicity within hours, prompting onlookers to wonder: *who is Tommy Hilfiger?*

Is it risky to claim you're one of the best designers in the world? You bet—but not nearly as risky as following the formula of models on a beach. It was a *calculated risk*. It certainly helped that Hilfiger was actually talented enough to back up the claim, but this assured people would still recognize his name, whether they liked his clothes or not.

Could that frozen yogurt shop make ends meet by keeping jalapenos and potato chips out of their frozen yogurt? Maybe. Would Tommy Hilfiger have risen to stardom without George Lois audaciously positioning him as the next great American designer? We'll never know. But both know understand something very important:

the worst fate for a brand isn't a nasty reputation or a dip in sales—it's being ignored.

-|-

In the beginning of this chapter, we mentioned that taking risks raises a lot of questions. Is it worth risking your reputation? When is a risk actually a risk? Is all publicity good publicity? The honest (but disappointing) answer to those questions and more is, *it depends*. Some marketers might take a binary view towards risk—either it's always awesome or always dumb. But in case you forgot the point of this entire book, marketing isn't science or math, it's art—and with art comes no shortage of nuance.

So What?

1. Risk is worthless without execution. Don't just talk the talk.

2. If a marketing decision feels radical, you might be paying too much attention to the competition rather than the audience.

3. If you're on the fence about risk, remember that failure isn't as painful as being forgotten.

CHAPTER 6

Getting Un-F!!cked

In 2006, neuroscientists in London discovered a startling difference between the brains of taxi drivers and bus drivers. After analyzing dozens of MRI scans, the researchers found that the cab drivers had significantly more "gray matter" in their hippocampuses (the area at the base of the brain) compared to their bus-driving counterparts. Quite literally, the cabbies had bigger brains.

As you can imagine, this finding raised plenty of hotly-debated questions. Were bus drivers inherently dumb? Were cabbies an unusually intelligent bunch? Or was this just one giant fluke? The answer turned out to be quite simple, and opened the floodgates for a new discussion about how the human brain works.

Taxi drivers in London are required to learn 320 different route combinations within a six-mile radius that entails a mind-boggling 25,000 streets. Cabbies are under constant pressure to navigate bustling streets in the shortest amount of time for impatient riders. Bus drivers, on the other hand, only have to follow a limited set of predetermined routes. They repeat the same drive over and over every day. Obviously, the latter is an easier gig, but you pay the price in the form of a shriveled hippocampus.

For centuries, it was assumed that as human beings aged, the connections in their brains solidified. The adage "You can't teach an old dog new tricks" suggested that learning and adapting is a young person's game. However, the London cabbie study (and others) all but proved the modern theory of neuroplasticity, which refers to the brain's ability to reorganize itself by forming new connections, regardless of age. You octogenarians out there who are thinking about learning French, **simplement fais-le!** (Just do it).

So, what does neuroplasticity have to do with marketing? As we've explored throughout the past five chapters, business folk—especially marketers—are wired to think with formulas. It starts in college with memorizing mundane marketing terminology like "The 5 Ps" and bleeds into the corporate world where we're hammered over the head with conflicting tricks, tips, and best practices. This plug-and-play marketing philosophy puts our brains on auto-pilot, making us content to simply go through the motions. We've witnessed this ad nauseum throughout our careers. It sucks.

But there's hope.

Similar to cab drivers growing their brains by adapting to new routes, marketers can expand their creative horizons and liberate themselves from the tyranny of formulaic thinking. But how?

As much as we'd love to give you a metaphorical "reset" button to unlearn your college marketing textbooks or that Gary Vee podcast you listened to on the way to work, it's not that easy. There are, however, exercises that can spark independent thinking. While many marketing books, courses, and articles focus on finding "the answer," we're more concerned with the mentality that **leads to your own answer**. Just like those 320 route combinations force cabbies to always be on the edge of their seats (literally), these five exercises can help you cultivate a mindset that challenges formulas rather than accepting them.

Kill Your Company

In 2000, Netflix founder Reed Hastings approached former Blockbuster CEO John Antioco. Hastings offered to sell his fledgling company—then an on-demand DVD mailing service—for $50 million. Antioco passed on the deal under the impression that Netflix was a small, niche business.

Within two years Netflix went public, soared past Blockbuster, and ultimately wrote the brick-and-mortar movie store's death sentence. Actually, there is one lonely Blockbuster store still standing in Bend, Oregon. But it's more of a destination for bearded hipsters carrying 35mm cameras than families looking to rent DVDs.

We can only imagine the cringes that ensure every time John Antioco hears the phrase "online streaming." Of course, Blockbuster isn't the only brand that's had its lunch eaten by up-and-comers. Pan-Am used to be America's largest airline. BlackBerry was once the fastest growing company in the world. But as we all know, Southwest Airlines and Apple stepped on their respective scenes to shatter the status quo.

These sudden, dramatic overtakings are proof that survival and adaptation go hand-in-hand. If you're not on the lookout for external threats to your sacred strategies, you'll be defenseless once they start breathing down your neck. Fortunately, there's a powerful exercise that can reframe your perspective and identify flawed ideas—and it all starts with asking yourself or your team a simple question:

What would you do to put us out of business today?

By switching your mindset from defense to offense with this "kill the company" exercise, you open up the floodgates for new ideas that could crush your brand. But instead of falling victim to those ideas, you adopt them as your own (so long as they're viable).

The first time HBO conducted a kill-the-company exercise, it generated three pages full of tactics that a rival network might use to destroy their brand: new shows, media strategies, the list went on. Pharmaceutical giant Merck uses the exercise to identify new, untapped markets and drugs. And marketers can "kill their campaigns" to find weak spots or kick their creativity up a notch. After all, your competitors are doing that anyway.

"The competition doesn't care about manners or stepping on egos," says Lisa Bodell, author of *Kill the Company: End the Status Quo, Start an Innovation Revolution*. "It just wants to get to the big opportunities before you do."

A lack of urgency is among the most notorious threats to improvement and innovation. But plotting the demise of your cherished idea? That lights a fire under your team's ass that's sure to jumpstart any brainstorm.

Find the First Principles

Imagine you have these three items:

- A bulldozer
- A motorboat pulling a skier
- A bicycle

If you were asked what you could create with these at your disposal, you might be puzzled. That's understandable. The bulldozer, motorboat, and bicycle exist as separate entities. Messing with them wouldn't make them any more useful than they already are. But what if I asked what you could create with this list of supplies:

- A tread kit
- Steel armor plates
- A motor
- Skis
- Handlebars

For starters, you could build a snowmobile. Now, you also could have built a snowmobile with the items in the first list, but the names probably threw you off. It wasn't until those items were separated into their individual parts that it made sense to create something original. This is an example of "first principles thinking" (also known as reasoning from first principles) which is the act of boiling a process or problem down to individual components and reassembling them to build a better solution. First principle thinking has been used by geniuses from Aristotle to Elon Musk in order to stimulate independent thinking. The good news is marketers can reap the benefits of first principle thinking as well.

In 1440, Johannes Gutenberg had on his resume a university education and an apprenticeship with a goldsmith. Printing was a cumbersome process, so Gutenberg went way out of the box and looked to a wine press for inspiration. He cobbled together a screw press, movable type, paper, and ink to create the first printing press. Inventors aren't the only people who can benefit from this way of thinking. Marketers can borrow insights from other disciplines and remix them with any number of old and new ideas to create custom solutions. There's no reason why we should be confined to the rules, formulas, or templates that are so deeply ingrained into marketing culture. I've always found that marketing strategies tend to work better when you treat them like Play Doh instead of concrete.

I touched on this briefly in chapter four when we explored shiny object syndrome. Rather than accepting a solution on a silver platter, break it down into its individual components. What can you do with a hint of this or a pinch of that? What can you toss out? What is essential? Paradoxically, breaking ideas into pieces makes them easier to manage than simply trying to replicate them. Our tendency to imitate ideas we admire is precisely the roadblock that inhibits genuine creative thinking. The famous Einstein quote, while cliche, nails it: "Insanity is doing the same thing over and over again and expecting a different result."

It may seem ironic, but the simplest way to progress might be to *re*gress to the basics—and then rebuild.

Find (Don't Appoint) a Devil's Advocate

When Polaroid co-founder Edwin Land introduced the world's first instant camera in 1948, his company started printing more than pictures—it was printing money as well. Within a decade, Polaroid's revenues surged from $7 million to nearly $100 million. By 1976, revenues reached towards $1 billion. But as the digital photography revolution got underway, Polaroid's progress came to a screeching halt.

In 1980, Sony founder Akio Morita reached out to Land about collaborating on an electronic camera. Land scoffed at the idea of pixels replacing film and insisted that the quality of digital pictures could never match that of chemically processed photographs. But his obstinance didn't stop there. As Polaroid withered in the face of digital disruption, Land shielded himself from all traces of dissent. "He surrounded himself with devoted followers who would do his bidding," said one longtime colleague. Land went as far as moving to a separate floor at Polaroid's headquarters where naysayers were denied access. Fast forward to 2001, and Polaroid was officially bankrupt.

How could Edwin Land turn a blind eye toward digital photography for two decades? It clearly wasn't just a passing fad. This is far from an isolated incident. We all have a tendency to put on blinders and attempt to spare ourselves from the thought that our cherished ideas are faulty. So, is there an antidote? Or are we doomed to perpetually fall victim to our own egos?

If you ask psychologist Charlan Nemeth, the solution starts with seeking negative feedback. In her book, **In Defense of Trouble-makers**, Nemeth points out that we must go beyond the notion of just appointing a devil's advocate to point out hypothetical problems. We must engage with people who genuinely and wholeheartedly disagree with us.

"Minority viewpoints are important, not because they tend to prevail but because they stimulate divergent attention and thought," says Nemeth. "As a result, even when they are wrong they contribute to the detection of novel solutions and decisions that, on balance, are qualitatively better."

Nemeth's insight was reflected in a study by strategy researchers Michael McDonals and James Westphal which found that the more CEOs sought advice from friends and colleagues who shared their opinions, the worse their companies performed. Company performance only improved when those CEOs considered advice from outsiders who held their feet to the fire and challenged them to reconsider their assumptions.

Over the years, it's become increasingly obvious that the more I remove my ego from a situation, the better the results. In most instances, that means giving more weight to the audience I'm trying to reach and what matters to them rather than my own pride. If I need to help a brand engage with 22-year-old women, there's a good chance my instincts will be way off base since I'm a 48-year-old dude. That's where the devil's advocate comes in.

Instead of gambling with my gut feeling, I'd rather talk to someone who can call me on my bullshit, especially if that person is a member of the target demographic. Will actively seeking out contrary opinions hurt your feelings? Probably. In fact, it's one of the hardest exercises to undertake as an adviser. But how else can you grow and learn?

Marketers with a track record of success often presume others think and believe exactly as they do without any substantiating evidence other than their buddy Earl or gal pal Jenna telling them as much. So, next time you think that all women will fall in love with your client's new pleated skirt designs, go seek out and speak to five women whom you have no ties to whatsoever and ask them to put your ideas to the test.

Get Desperate

In 2011, HBO ran a program called *Talking Funny* featuring comedians Louis CK, Jerry Seinfield, Chris Rock and Ricky Gervais. These modern standup legends discussed how important comedy was to them and what it takes to make it to the top of the totem pole. If you're an aspiring comedian, it's a must-watch. But if you don't have time, I'll share one of the most interesting insights which came from Louis CK (prior to his scandal).

To force himself to improve, Louis CK wouldn't just write a brand new set every year—he'd also open his new act with his strongest bit from the previous year's act. Typically, comedians save their best bit for last, so by shuffling his best bits to the top every year, he was forced to continually write better material.

"One of the things I started doing when I was developing my hours is I'd take my closing bit, and I'd open with it. Just to f–k myself [so I'd be forced] to follow my strongest bit," he said. "You get rid of all your best weapons and you have to [rise to the occasion] or else your dead. It brings something out of you."

That remark impressed Jerry Seinfeld, who looked to Chris Rock and said, "*That's how he got good.* You see this attitude—he's a tough guy."

This got me thinking: What if agencies and brands held themselves to the same standard? What if we frontloaded our best ideas to force ourselves to innovate and improve? As I reflected on that parallel, it became clear that it might be exactly the shot in the arm our industry needs to bust out of its shell.

Many marketers use time as a crutch. We might imagine that there will be time to think of a better idea tomorrow. Maybe we're waiting for someone to knock on our door with the next big idea on a silver platter. But this mentality is the biggest obstacle to innovation. Some of the best innovations have been developed out of desperation. "Necessity is the mother of invention," goes the proverb. Chronic back pain led to the invention of the tennis ball hopper. Cocoa shortages in Italy during World War II prompted chefs to add hazelnuts to desserts—the first iteration of Nutella.

The same principle applies to marketing: If you can't afford to lose, you won't. Don't wait for a competitor to hold your feet to the fire, do it yourself. Give your ideas away so you have to come up with better ones. Pitch your best concept first, so just like Louis CK, you're forced to go up from there. You'll be surprised how quickly your mind comes to life when the clock is ticking.

Don't Just Think Outside the Box— Think Outside the Industry

In 2013, a trio of professors from Denmark and Austria set out to answer a simple yet perplexing question: Where do novel ideas come from? This was prompted by a bizarre trend of highly qualified business managers having trouble coming up with innovative solutions to their own problems. The closer they were to their respective industries, the harder it seemed to think clearly.

The researchers asked hundreds of roofers, carpenters and inline skaters to solve the problem of reluctance to use safety equipment because of discomfort. The participants were asked questions about each field. For example, how could roofers' safety belts, carpenters' respirator masks, and skaters' knee pads be redesigned to improve comfort and increase use?

A panel of neutral analysts looked at the solutions and noticed something incredible. Each group devised significantly more creative ideas for other fields than for its own. What's more, the weaker the relationship between the two fields, the more creative the ideas were. The skaters' ideas about carpenters' masks were more innovative than the roofers' ideas and far more innovative than the carpenters' ideas about their own masks.

This finding wasn't just some hypothetical theory cooked up on a college campus. Consider 3M which developed a breakthrough concept to prevent surgical infections after receiving input from a theatrical-makeup artist. Or an escalator company that borrowed insights from the coal mining industry when figuring out how to install escalators in shopping malls.

Professor-types call this "analogous market problem solving," but forget the fancy semantics. The point is that you don't need to listen to your industry "experts" to formulate a creative solution—as the study demonstrated, that can easily backfire. Instead, you might just need a new pair of eyes on your situation.

Conventional wisdom would suggest that you need to know your industry like the back of your own hand in order to solve a business problem. But familiarity can often be a hindrance rather than a help. We're too mired in our own thoughts, habits and concerns to look at the situation from a fresh perspective. Think about how easy it is to offer relationship advice to your friend, but how complicated you make your own relationship issues. Perspective is everything.

"Look for creative people who aren't constrained by the assumed limitations and mental schemas of your own professional world," says Marion Poetz, one of the researchers for the safety gear study. "These are people who, although they know little of your field, may be more likely to come up with breakthrough thinking; indeed, they may be carrying around, in their heads, the germ of the solution you've been searching for all along."

–|–

We've said it throughout the book and we'll say it again: Don't take this stuff verbatim. The lessons you just read aren't a plug-and-play or a copy-and-paste type of deal. They're intended to get you out of a rut, think for yourself, and help you come up with a solution that's right *for you and you only*. We both hate being told how to think as much as the next guy, but don't think of this chapter as five "rules." Think of it as five nudges to open up your mind to a world of possibilities.

So What?

1. What's a campaign that a competitor could launch to put your brand out business? Think about that, and go one step better.

2. Actively seek out people who disagree with you. Your ego is your enemy.

3. Creative ideas often come from industries outside of your own. Don't just ask your neighbors for help. Go to a different city altogether.

4. A sense of urgency is the greatest motivator to come up with new ideas. If you can't afford to lose, you won't.

Conclusion: There's a Better Way

A conclusionary conclusion would conclude that a business book conclude with a conclusion. With that said, allow us to pose a controversial statement: There's a good chance you've been eating cupcakes the wrong way your entire life.

Wait, what?

Indeed, since cupcakes first gained prominence in the late 1700s, eager eaters have thoughtlessly stuffed their mouths, leaving their cheeks smeared with icing and sprinkles lodged in the depths of their noses. It's a beautifully barbaric act of eating. But as it turns out, there's a better way to eat cupcakes—one that lets you enjoy them without inhaling them through your nostrils while maintaining the perfect frosting-to-cake ratio.

It starts by twisting or cutting the cupcake in half. Next, simply stack the bottom half of on top of the icing and smush it together. This creates a cupcake sandwich that spares you from having to go through an entire pack of napkins. No mess, all the deliciousness. This is game-changing stuff, folks.

Food hacks don't stop with cupcakes, though. You can peel a banana easier from the bottom, rather than the stem. You can make better use of paper ketchup cups by fanning them out for a wider dunking radius. And you can peel a mango in less than ten seconds with a household glass.

The point is there's ***always*** a better way—whether it's how you consume baked goods or how you grow a brand. Unfortunately many people are so preoccupied with preserving the status quo that they never think look beyond what's lying right in front of them. But once you cultivate the mindset of a relentless improver, you'll never look at anything the same way—including cupcakes.

The Fault in the Default Settings

In 2013, economist Michael Housman set out to discover why some employees stayed at their jobs longer than their coworkers. Armed with data from more than 30,000 people, he explored a variety of factors that he suspected were contributing to serial job hopping: poor relationships, bad attitude, and so on. But as Housman dug deeper, he noticed something strange. There was a correlation between the internet browser that employees used and their job retention rate: Employees who used Firefox or Chrome kept their jobs 15 percent longer than those who used Internet Explorer or Safari.

But it wasn't just retention that was impacted. The Firefox and Chrome users were also less likely to miss work, performed better, and achieved higher customer satisfaction levels compared to the Explorer and Safari users. This couldn't be more than a coincidence, thought Housman. How could an internet browser enhance job retention and performance?

As it turns out, the browser itself has nothing to do with showing up to work or succeeding. Rather, it's what an employee's browser preference **signals about their character**. If you have a PC, Internet Explorer is the default internet browser. If you have a Mac, Safari comes preinstalled. To get Firefox or Chrome, however, you have to take the initiative to find a better option. Instead of accepting the default setting, you seek out an upgrade.

"That act of initiative, however tiny, is a window into what you do at work," says psychologist Adam Grant in his book *Originals: How Non-Conformists Move the World*.

The employees who accepted the defaults on their computers were the same employees who accepted the defaults in their careers: They failed to take initiative, became stagnant, grew dissatisfied, and quit. The Firefox and Chrome users, on the other hand, were always on the lookout for improvement. Put simply, they wrote their own script instead of following the one they were handed.

"We live in an Internet Explorer world," says Grant. "Justifying the default system serves a soothing function. It's an emotional painkiller: If the world is supposed to be this way, we don't need to be dissatisfied with it. But acquiescence also robs us of the moral outrage to stand against injustice and the creative will to consider alternative ways that the world could work."

This statement remains true whether it's applied to the world of marketing, medicine, or music. Grooving with the status quo has always been easy and always will be. But the people who pave new paths are ultimately the ones who determine its direction. Unfortunately, these people are the exception rather than the rule.

Viva La Idea

When we launched Elasticity in 2009, we emblazoned "Viva La Idea" on the logo of our mustached robot. Why? To answer that question, let's talk about the core of what an agency is. There are countless cogs that make an agency work and countless ways through which an agency can make a name for itself. Most will say it's their people. You may also hear about processes, tools, client lists and otherwise. But really, it comes down to *ideas*.

If you're in marketing, you've most likely been part of a few brainstorming sessions in your day. These meetings are generally where ideas are created—and killed. I'll never forget one I was in and right after I voiced an out-of-the-box idea, my old boss Tim said, "Well there are no bad ideas in a brainstorm. Who else has something?"

And if unique ideas don't die in brainstorms led by luddites, they have two more death traps to get past: the account manager and the client.

All too often, the pressure falls on account managers. They stress out about what they believe the client wants, and more likely, how much money the account brings into the agency. This might cause them to get squeamish at the thought of presenting an edgy idea, prompting him or her to shy away from standing up for that idea if the client is on the fence.

Believe it or not, clients want—and *need*—to hear that big idea, even if they won't buy it. Yes, the idea needs to be inline with the brand's culture. But forget the risk. It's possible to take a bold stance and not jeopardize your business, but rather gain respect because of it.

We started Elasticity because we stood behind the fact that clients deserve more than what's drummed up in most agencies. We grew sick and tired of tools and tactics passing as "strategies." So, for the creative talent that watches good ideas die every day, for the clients that miss out on groundbreaking campaigns due to complacency, and for the ideas themselves, we pledged to create and embrace kick-ass ideas. And believe me when I say kick-ass ideas can come from anybody. It doesn't matter if you're an intern or collecting social security, whether you have one year or 30 years under your belt, whether you are black or white, like boys or girls, if you're into breakdancing or the waltz, enjoy eating meat or only veggies. Bring it. Viva La Idea.

You might be familiar with the phrase "Big Hairy Audacious Goal." If not, here's a recap from Wikipedia:

"The term 'Big Hairy Audacious Goal' (BHAG) was proposed by James Collins and Jerry Porras in their 1994 book *Built to Last: Successful Habits of Visionary Companies*. A BHAG encourages companies to define visionary goals that are more strategic and emotionally compelling. A Big Hairy Audacious Goal is a strategic business statement created to focus an organization on a single medium-long term organization-wide goal which is audacious, likely to be externally questionable, but not internally regarded as impossible."

Here are a few real life examples of BHAGs:

- Amazon: Make every book ever printed in any language available at the touch of a button.
- Google: Organize the world's information and make it universally accessible and useful.
- Microsoft: Put a computer on every desk and in every home.

Even if these brands didn't fulfill their visions, it's the mindset that matters most. It's extremely hard to justify hard work if there is no underlying mission that gets you fired up. The same principle applies to marketing efforts. *Every* campaign should have it's own BHAG. No CMO or any agency pitching a campaign should settle for anything less than something big, hairy, and audacious—end of discussion. Otherwise, why do it?

Pitching **The New York Times** is not a BHAG. Starting a podcast is not a BHAG. Instagram story ads are not a BHAG. Pitching Canada Dry on creating an annual World Ginger Appreciation Day where every redhead gets a free six-pack of ginger ale and a hug—now *that's* a BHAG.

We need bigger goals, ones that make us say "Can we actually do that?" and make onlookers do a double-take. If your team disagrees, it's up to you to change their mind—or find a new team. Pushing boundaries and breaking rules might cause you to be criticized, laughed out of a room, or even fired. But you won't be ignored.

-|-

Acknowledgments

I was informed this is the part of the book where I'm supposed to thank everyone in my life who inspired me to write this riveting—and now certainly best-selling—literary masterpiece. Whether you've actually read this far or just skipped ahead to gauge my humility, I applaud your effort.

I owe a debt of gratitude to my wife, Susan Perlut, for tolerating my rugged good looks and my never-ending omniscience. I'm also grateful for my sons, Jackson and Trey, who have little-to-no interest in my career nor this book. Rounding out my immediate family, thanks to my parents for completely screwing up my mind.

I'd like to thank my former boss, Tim, and old white men everywhere for inspiring me to not be like them in any way, shape or form. Speaking of white guys named Tim, thank you Tim Cook and Apple for making wireless earbuds so that I can find amusement in those who wear them (sorry, Brian). Thanks to William D. Johnson and Howard Keith Poston for being tall. Thanks to ALF for, "Ha, Willie!" Thanks to pants and bacon.

I'd be remiss if I didn't acknowledge my deep-seated insecurity and alcohol for driving nearly every poor choice I've ever made. Shout out to people of Ginger descent everywhere, especially the barista whom I offended in June of 2019. Keep on keepin' on. I greatly appreciate the sage advice of Mr. T and his willingness to pity fools, because I need your pity.

And last but not least, thank you to all Elasticians—past, present and future—for constantly kicking ass, tolerating my toxic masculinity, and making Elasticity a remarkably remarkable place to work. Even you, Zach.

You know I love you all. Don't make me say it in a book. But, seriously, I had hair before I knew you all. So there's that. But thank you, anyway. Where are the soft cookies again?

About the Authors

Aaron Perlut is the co-founder, managing partner and chief pork and mustache strategist of Elasticity. A former senior Omnicom (FleishmanHillard) counselor and communications executive for two of the nation's largest energy companies, Aaron has spent more than 20 years in media and marketing helping a range of organizations—from Fortune 500s to professional sports franchises to startups to nonprofits—manage reputation and market brands in an evolving media environment.

Brian Cross is the co-founder, managing partner and director of rocket science at Elasticity. Brian was previously the global practice group lead for FleishmanHillard's digital communications practice and has worked with brands including AT&T, Yahoo!, Papa John's and Visa. At Elasticity, Brian is responsible for leading innovation in digital communications impacting online word of mouth, public outreach, and social media.

Made in the USA
Monee, IL
07 December 2020

51520352R00079